ISBN 978-1-331-12694-2
PIBN 10148378

1 MONTH OF
FREE
READING

at

www.ForgottenBooks.com

By purchasing this book you are eligible for one month membership to ForgottenBooks.com, giving you unlimited access to our entire collection of over 1,000,000 titles via our web site and mobile apps.

To claim your free month visit:

www.forgottenbooks.com/free148378

"THE BASIS OF OUR POLITICAL SYSTEMS IS THE RIGHT OF THE PEOPLE TO MAKE AND ALTER THEIR CONSTITUTIONS OF GOVERNMENT."—WASHINGTON.

See also the Constitution of Rhode Island, Art. I, Sec. I.

CONSTITUTION - MAKING IN RHODE ISLAND

AMASA M. EATON, A.M., LL.B.

This contribution to the discussion concerning "Constitution-making in Rhode Island" is published by the RHODE ISLAND CONSTITUTIONAL LEAGUE; but the League, though earnestly concurring in the arguments advanced as to the proper and legal way to make a new constitution for our State, does not hold itself responsible for, nor committed to, every view or conclusion therein expressed.

PROVIDENCE, R. I.

1899

PRESS OF
E. L. FREEMAN & SONS,
PROVIDENCE, R. I.

CONTENTS.

9. A provision in a constitution limiting the power of the majority to alter it would be void.

Art. XIII reconcilable with this, because it relates only to amendments and was to provide against a hasty change.

This is rather an excuse than a defence.

It is a mistake to undertake to prevent a majority from rewriting or amending their constitution.

10. If a distinction is made, the party in power will adopt the course most likely to carry out their aim.

The "Revised Constitution" so-called, by legal fiction, was really a new constitution.

It reversed the distinction between Art. I, Sec. 1, and Art. XIII of the present constitution.

It put the will of the general assembly above the will of the people.

It put it in the hands of the party in power to adopt the course the most likely to subserve their ends.

11. Constitutions are too sacred to be framed so they can be thus juggled with.

To prevent it, the majority should govern, however a change in the constitution is instituted.

The fundamental principle of all Anglo-Saxon government is that the majority rule when its will is ascertained through the forms prescribed to that end.

This is what Washington meant in his language quoted in Art. I, Sec. 1.

While power of general assembly to propose amendments can be limited, no limitations can be imposed upon right of people to make and alter their constitution of government.

Except a vote of majority of all the electors might be made requisite.

No State has yet done this.

Necessity for vote of more than bare majority to change constitution is defended to prevent hasty action.

Such a claim involves want of faith inconsistent with faith in our system of government.

12. The majority rules in England, without our guarantees of a written constitution.

In this State this want of faith is relic of policy of Anti-Dorrites.

The principles Dorr contended for were right.

His error was in appealing to arms.

The principal should be adopted that the majority shall rule when their will is ascertained in a lawful, explicit, and authentic manner.

To deny it is to establish an obligarchic form of governmont;

    One inconsistent with Art. IV, Sec. 4, constitution of the United States.

It is not a republican form of government if the majority cannot make or alter their constitution of government.

A republican form of government is one in which the majority governs.

That our forefathers in this State intended the majority should govern is evident from examination of their compacts of government.

13. These compacts examined :

B

PREFACE.

In reply to questions put by the senate, the members of the supreme court gave their advisory opinion March 30, 1883, to the effect that the general assembly has no power to call a constitutional convention. If correct, this would render wholly nugatory the express declaration contained in Article I, section 1, of the constitution: "The basis of our political systems is the right of the people to make and alter their constitutions of government." January 27, 1897, the general assembly passed a resolution "stating there is a wide-spread feeling among the people of the State that the constitution should be carefully and thoroughly revised, and such changes as may seem to be advisable, in view of the changed condition since it was adopted, properly and carefully prepared," and, therefore, authorizing the governor to appoint a commission of fifteen persons to revise the constitution and to make report to the general assembly, that such revised constitution might be submitted to the electors in the form of an amendment to the present constitution. The governor appointed the commission, in accordance with the authority thus conferred upon him. This commission made report to the general assembly at its January session, 1898, submitting a revised constitution drawn by them. This revised constitution was submitted by the general assembly to the electors of the State as an amendment to the existing constitution under Article XIII thereof, and failed to receive the necessary approval of three-fifths. It was again submitted to the electors on June 20, 1899, with a change of the time a constitutional convention should be called, and again it failed to pass. It would seem, therefore, that despite the admitted necessity for a new constitution none is to be had. It is the purpose of this pamphlet to show that the general assembly should call a constitutional convention forthwith; that it has this power; that the advisory opinion to the contrary was clearly wrong and has no effect as a judicial decision; that this course would be strictly in accordance with established American usage, when necessity arises for a revision of the constitution; that such thorough revision can be made in no other way; that the majority always has the right and power to make and alter the constitution; that this doctrine is strictly in accord with the provisions of the existing constitution and of Article I, section 1, more particularly; that the constitution framed by this convention should be submitted to the vote of the electors, including those who will become electors under it, and should become the law of the land if approved by a majority of those voting thereon, as was the case, in both respects, when the existing constitution was adopted in 1842. It is further the purpose of this pamphlet to show some of the defects and omissions of the existing constitution and how they may be remedied, submitting to that end an essay at a draft of a new constitution for the consideration of those who wish to see the government of this State made what it should be, in the hope that this may in some degree contribute to that end.

AMASA M. EATON.

Providence, R. I., September 19, 1899.

PETITION TO GENERAL ASSEMBLY.

To the Honorable the General Assembly:

The Constitutional League respectfully represents:

In the words of the resolution passed by the general assembly, January 27, 1897:

"There is a wide-spread feeling among the people of the State that the constitution should be carefully and thoroughly revised, and such changes as may seem to be advisable, in view of the changed condition of affairs since it was adopted, properly and carefully prepared."

Art. I, sec. 1 of our constitution expressly declares, in the words of the Father of his Country, that "the basis of our political system is the right of the people to make and alter their constitutions of government, but that the constitution which at any time exists, till changed by an explicit and authentic act of the whole people, is sacredly obligatory upon all."

The time has come for a change by an explicit and authentic act of the whole people, and this can only be done through a constitutional convention, composed of delegates lawfully elected for that purpose, the result of the labors of such convention to be submitted to the electors for approval or rejection. This method is consonant with our system of government, and is the method usually followed in the States of our Union.

If elaborate express provisions had been inserted in the constitution, providing how this right of the people to make and alter their constitutions of government could be carried into effect, no implication found by construction in any other clause of the constitution could be held to deprive the people of this expressly stated right and power to make and alter their constitutions of government.

We submit that the absence of such provisions does not render any the less secure and absolute this expressly stated right. Details of this kind are properly omitted from a written constitution, the law-making branch of the government being the proper one to carry into effect the principles stated, and the powers and rights granted or reserved, by appropriate legislation or action.

This league, therefore, respectfully petitions your honorable body to call a constitutional convention to frame a new constitution that shall be submitted to the electors for their approval or disapproval.

But it will be claimed it has been decided by the justices of the supreme court that the general assembly has no power to call a constitutional convention, because they have said so in their advisory opinion.

This were to ignore the recognized distinction between an *advisory opinion* of the judges and an *actual decision* of a litigated case by the court, and to treat the opinion as an actual decision. This is the common device of those who, not wanting a constitutional convention, shelter themselves behind this false shield. Having such profound deference for the court, why do they not also defer to the court's own declaration and recognition of the distinction pointed out?

In the case of Allen *vs.* Danielson, reported in 15 R. I. 480, after a full hearing, with arguments and citation of authorities on both sides, the judges, as a court, reversed their own advisory opinion as members of the court, on the same subject, reported in 13 R. I. 9, giving as one of their reasons for doing so, the fact that the question in 13 R. I. 9 "was a petition on a case stated, and was doubtless submitted without full argument or presentation of authorities. * * * * * But we have no doubt that we should have decided the case differently if we had had before us, when we decided it, the same array of authorities which we have before us now."

In Taylor *vs.* Place, 4 R. I. 324, the same question came before the supreme court, in an actual case, that the judges had previously given a written opinion upon, to the governor. The court, by Ames, C. J., said: "This is the first time, since the adoption of the constitution, that this question has been brought judicially to the attention of the court. The advice or opinion given by the judges of this court, when requested, to the governor, or to either house of the assembly, under the third section of the tenth article of the constitution, is not a decision of this court; and given as it must be, without the aid which the court derives in adversary cases from able and experienced counsel, though it may afford much light from the reasonings or research displayed in it, can have no weight as a precedent."

The supreme court of this State has, therefore, decided twice that an advisory opinion of its members is not conclusive, and may be reversed when the same matter comes before the court in an actual case.

Twenty-seven constitutional conventions have been called by the State legislatures, acting without specific authority in the respective existing constitutions to call such a convention. Thirteen of these occurred before the constitution of this State was adopted, in 1842. Of the original thirteen States only one contained a provision for amendment, yet all have changed their constitutions, and all have done it through constitutional conventions called by the legislature. The common practice of these and of other States has fixed this as a part of the common constitutional law of the land.

The framers of our constitution, in omitting to prescribe how a constitutional convention may be called, knew, or may be supposed to have known, this prevailing custom of calling such conventions by State legislatures, without specific authority so to do in the existing constitutions, and, therefore, they did not deem it necessary to do more than to affirm the right of the people to make and alter their constitutions of government, leaving it to the general assembly to give effect to this expressly reserved right, by appropriate action, whenever the necessity might arise.

This league adopts a construction that gives effect both to Article I, section 1, and to Article XIII of the constitution. It gives effect thereby to the absolute and unlimited right of a majority of the people to make and alter their constitutions of government, as expressly stated in Article I, section 1. It gives effect, also, thereby to Article XIII, stating the limited manner in which one branch of the government, the general assembly, may initiate amendments to the constitution. But for the express limitation upon the power of the general assembly therein contained, the usual majority of the general assembly could propose amendments for the approval of the usual majority of the electors. They are forbidden to do so, except by a majority of all the members elected to each house in two successive general assemblies. A self-imposed limitation is also placed upon the power of the electors, preventing them from acting by the usual majority, and requiring the assent of three-fifths of the electors voting thereon, before any amendment thus proposed shall become a part of the constitution. To extend Article XIII by implication into an abrogation of the express right reserved in Article I, section 1, is to violate the well-known rule of construction requiring effect to be given, if possible, to all the provisions of an instrument.

Instead of following this rule, the advisory opinion of the judges enlarges the scope and operation of Article XIII beyond anything ever contemplated by its framers, makes it exclusive by what it thus finds implied in it, and thereby entirely abrogates and excludes Article I section 1, thus depriving the people of their expressly reserved right to make and alter their constitutions of government. It is not thus that constitutional guarantees are to be construed.

In view of these facts and principles, still insisting that the general assembly has power to call a constitutional convention, the necessity therefor being generally as well as officially admitted, that the advisory opinion denying this right is clearly erroneous, and that in no event does it have force and effect as a decision, we respectfully petition your honorable body to call a constitutional convention; or, if the power to do so be still doubted, we ask that these important questions be again submitted to the members of the supreme court, with an opportunity such as the judges themselves said in their advisory opinion they would be glad to have, to give them more careful study, and especially with opportunity for the presentation to the judges of all views relating thereto, with full argument and presentation of authorities, in order that the conclusions reached may merit the confidence, approval, and support of the people of the State.

But should the general assembly in its wisdom deem either of these courses inadvisable, we respectfully petition your honorable body to submit to the electors an amendment to the constitution providing for calling a constitutional convention, under and in accordance with the provisions of Article XIII of the constitution, and providing that the constitution drafted by such convention shall go into effect if approved by a majority of the electors voting thereon, such electors to include those who will become electors under such new constitution, following in these particulars the precedent set upon the submission and adoption of the existing constitution in 1842. And as in duty bound your petitioners will ever pray.

THE CONSTITUTIONAL LEAGUE,

H. J. SPOONER, *President.*
ARTHUR W. BROWN, *Secretary,*

AMASA M. EATON,
DANIEL R. BALLOU,
J. Q. DEALEY,
EDWARD D. BASSETT,
} *Committee.*

CONSTITUTION-MAKING IN RHODE ISLAND.

Article I, section 1, of the constitution of Rhode Island begins: "In the words of the Father of his Country, we declare that 'the basis of our political systems is the right of the people to make and alter their constitutions of government' * * * * * * * * *."

The right of the people to make and alter their constitution of government could not be more expressly stated nor more explicitly reserved.

It is an unqualified absolute right—one, indeed, that exists even if not stated, for the same power that made our constitution, *i. e.* the sovereign people, can unmake it—can destroy it – can alter it.

But the makers of our constitution did not rely upon this undoubted sovereign power—the power to make and alter their constitution of government. They put it in the front of the written constitution, as the very right of all rights.

Nothing can deny nor destroy it. It is there, fixed and unalterable, and it only remains to give it force and effect. This might have been done by inserting a clause in the constitution providing the means for carrying it into effect.

We search in vain, however, throughout the rest of the constitution for any directions of this nature. We find it absolutely silent on the subject. There is the inherent right of the people that made the constitution to alter it, as well as to make it, expressly stated—but nothing more. The usual rule of construing such statements of rights and express reservations of powers in a written constitution is to give them full force and effect by broad construction and interpretation. Their scope is not to be narrowed by implication nor restriction, but they are to be enlarged and given full effect in securing the freedom of the subject and the preservation of his rights and privileges with all the consequences flowing therefrom. It is in this spirit that all the other statements of rights in our bills of rights are always construed and carried into effect.

In pursuance of this general policy of the law, it has always been held that the legislature has the power to pass laws to carry into effect the powers granted or reserved in the bill of rights of every constitution in the United States. The general assembly of this State has, therefore, the power to pass all legislation necessary to give effect to this expressly reserved right of the people to make and alter their constitution of government. One of the most appropriate, natural, and common means to effect this end is the issuance of a call to the people of the State to elect delegates to meet in convention to make such alterations in the constitution as may be necessary, and to submit the result of their labors to the approval or disapproval of the electors, when a necessity arises for revising the constitution. As necessary means to this end the general assembly may provide the time, mode, and manner for the election of such delegates and for the submission of their labors to the electors, and, if their vote be in the affirmative, the time when the new constitution shall take effect.

These are implied powers of the general assembly in the premises, resulting from the general grant of legislative powers to this department of government and the inherent indefeasible right of the sovereign power, the people, to make and alter their constitution of government, that, as it happens, in this State, is also, in the written constitution, an expressly stated right.

Whenever, therefore, the general assembly is satisfied that it is time a new constitution should be framed, it has the right and the power, nay, more, it becomes its duty, to call a constitutional convention. There can be no question that the time has come when a new constitution is demanded. It is a matter of common knowledge that public opinion has for years called for a new constitution. The general assembly has recognized the necessity by consideration of the subject year after year, by the question put to the judges in 1883 whether the general assembly can call a constitutional convention and by authorizing the appointment in 1897 by the governor of a commission to draft a new constitution by amending the old one, and by resolving January 27, 1897:

" There is a wide spread feeling among the people of the state that the constitution should be carefully and thoroughly revised, and such changes as may seem to be advisable, in view of the changed condition of affairs since it was adopted, properly and carefully prepared."

The right of the people to make and alter their constitution of government being absolute and being expressly stated, no limitation can be placed upon it by finding such a limitation implied in another clause of the constitution.

Hence, to contend that this right can only be exercised after the proposal of an amendment by the majority of all the members elected to each house of two successive general assemblies, etc., would be to place an implied limitation in the declaration made in Art. I, Sec. 1, by the makers of our constitution.

Let us see how it would read: "The basis of our political systems is the right of the people to make and alter their constitutions of government: *Provided, however*, this right of the people is subject to the will of the general assembly in the manner provided in Art. XIII," that is to say, this expressly stated right of the people can only be exercised at the initiative of the general assembly, the people's agent and servant, in the manner prescribed in Art. XIII.

The absolute right expressly secured to the people (and this means a majority of the people) is to be defeated by an implication that what was meant was that it could not be exercised unless first proposed by a majority of all the members of each house of two successive general assemblies, and approved by a three-fifths majority of the electors. This is to substitute, first, the will of the general assembly for the will of the people; and, second, the will of three-fifths for the will of a majority of the people. Is it thus that expressly stated sovereign rights are to be hedged in by implication?

Rather should a way be sought to give effect to both clauses of the constitution, and this, it is submitted, can be easily done by restricting the operation of Art. XIII to the case of amendments proposed by the general assembly, leaving Art. I, Sec. 1, to apply to everything outside of such amendments proposed by the people's agent, the general assembly. Surely a construction is to be preferred that shall give full force and effect to both clauses of the constitution rather than a construction that shall extend the operation of one clause to the extinction of the other clause, especially when the effect is to enlarge by implication the power conferred in one upon the people's agent, the general assembly, while completely extinguishing the express power reserved in the other to the people in their sovereign capacity.

The power of the general assembly to call a constitutional assembly is also further established by the fact that it has frequently exercised the power, and without objection.

Thus, the general assembly called a constitutional convention in 1824. It called another in 1834, another in 1841, and still another in 1842. This last one framed our present constitution. In 1853 the general assembly submitted to the voters the question whether a convention should be called, and they answered, no. It then asked them if they desired a revision of the constitution, and again the answer was no.

It will be contended, however, that all these calls of the general assembly for conventions were before the adoption of the present constitution, and that, as the judges said in their opinion of March 30, 1883, 14 R. I., at p. 654, the provision for amendment in the present constitution is exclusive. In reply, it is submitted that Article XIII relates only to amendments through the initiative of the general assembly, and has nothing to do with Article I, Sec. 1, reserving expressly the right of the people (not of the general assembly) to make and alter their constitution of government. In this view Article XIII is something extraneous and additional to Article I, Sec. 1, providing, not how the *people* may make and alter their constitution of government, but how the *agent of the people*, the general assembly, may initiate or suggest amendments, and providing further what sanction by the people shall make such suggested amendments a part of the constitution.

These repeated acts of the general assembly, before the present constitution was adopted, in calling constitutional conventions, show that when this constitution was framed, with the express statement in it that the people have a right to make and alter their constitution of government without providing specifically how this was to be done, the framers of the constitution took it for granted that the general assembly could do what it had done before, *i. e.*, call a constitutional convention whenever the necessity might arise, especially as they took care to add (Article IV, Sec. 10) "The general assembly shall continue to exercise the powers they have heretofore exercised, unless prohibited in this constitution."

The constitution adopted in 1842 was the work of a majority. Plainly a majority now as well as then can make and alter their constitution of government.

Article XIII provides that an amendment that has been passed by two successive general assemblies, by a majority of all the members elected to each house, and is approved by three-fifths of the electors voting thereon, shall thereupon become operative as a part of the constitution.

Plainly this mode of amending the constitution upon the initiative of the general assembly has nothing to do with the right of the people to make and alter their constitution of government, and cannot, even by implication, be considered as limiting that right in any way, but rather as setting up another and an additional manner in which, by the initiative of the general assembly only, a change can be made in the constitution. How can the absolute power of the people be limited simply by express mention of the way in which one agent of the people can propose amendments? Suppose it had been another agent of the government that had been entrusted with this power. Suppose the constitution had provided that the governor or the supreme court could suggest or initiate amendments that should become operative when sanctioned by a three-fifths majority, by what rule of construction could this additional mode of amending the constitution be tortured into an implied negation of the expressly stated power of the people to make and alter their constitution of government? The very fact that any amendment initiated by the general assembly shall not become a part of the constitution until approved by three-fifths of those voting thereon, shows that it is not in pursuance or in the exercise of the expressly reserved power of the people to make and alter their constitution of government (by a majority vote) that an amendment may be adopted in this peculiar manner, but rather that it is something extraneous and in addition to this expressly reserved power.

It is to be noticed, also, that although there is the express proviso that an amendment passed by two successive general assemblies must be ratified by a three-fifths vote, there is no limitation placed in Art. I, Sec. 1, upon the right of the people to make and alter their constitution of government, except that it shall be the explicit and authentic act of the whole people. In the absence of any such limitation, it follows as a matter of course that the power must be exercised as all other political powers are exercised, that is, by a majority, just as the constitution of 1842 itself became operative when ratified by a majority.

The good sense of the framers of our constitution is shown by the fact that they did not attempt to place any limitation upon the power of the majority of the electors as the representatives of the people to make and alter their constitution of government, for, had they made any such attempt, it would have been futile. For the same power that made can unmake. The majority made the constitution in 1842. The majority could unmake it the next day, or any other day, or to-morrow, of course in an orderly, lawful manner. By this it is meant that just as the present constitution became operative when ratified by a majority vote of the electors, so a new constitution framed by a constitutional convention called by the general assembly will become operative when ratified in the same way by a majority vote of the electors. If it is asked, by a majority of what electors, the answer is, by a majority of the electors including those who will become qualified as electors under such new constitution. This is what happened when the present constitution was adopted. The Law and Order party struggled against this conclusion, but at last they accepted it, as, indeed, they were obliged to. In the case of a small electorate and a new constitution that greatly enlarges the electorate, if the question of its adoption be left only to the old electorate, no change would ever be made. The old electors vote always to retain their own special privileges. Our old charter was abrogated finally and the present constitution with its enlarged electorate was carried by the votes of the new electors—that is to say, it was carried by the aid of those who were not voters under the old system, but who became voters under the new system. It is admitted that in the last analysis the power rests with those who can command the greatest physical force—that is to say, with the majority. One of the reasons that has been always presented against woman suffrage is the difficulty that would arise were the majority in number, including women who are physically weak, to vote one way, while the majority in physical strength were to refuse to obey their vote. It is not an argument that carries weight, but the fact of its presentation illustrates the truth that after all it is the physical majority that governs, as expressed by the vote of the majority. And when we say that the people are sovereign we mean that their will as made manifest by the action of the majority of electors determines the action of the State. The cardinal underlying principle of all so-called Anglo-Saxon or Teutonic government is that the majority shall rule. We say that the sovereign power is indefeasible and illimitable, which means that it is impossible to prevent the rule of the majority. It is the majority, making its behests known through the ballot-box, that governs. This government by the majority is one of the attributes of sovereignty, that is to say, the sovereign power rules through this expression of the will of the majority. Jameson, in his great work on Constitutional Conventions, p. 20, defines sovereignty as indefeasible, that is to say, incapable of being defeated or abrogated. Hence the sovereign right or power of government through the will of the people, as made known by the vote of a majority of the electors at the polls, is incapable of being abrogated or defeated.

The sovereign is the person or body of persons over whom there is politically no superior. (Jameson, Sec. 18.)

Penhallow v. Doane's Adr. 3 Dallas, 54.

"Sovereignty is and remains in the people."

It is inalienable—that is,

"Society can never delegate or pledge away sovereignty."

"Being inherent and necessarily in the State, it cannot pass from it so long as the latter exists." (Lieber Pol. Ethics, 250-251.)

A sovereign power, though it may temporarily place limitations upon the exercise of its own power, can, at any time, resume the exercise thereof untrammeled by its own self-imposed limitations. The limitations placed by a sovereign power upon the exercise of its own powers are not binding upon itself except in so far as it may choose to obey them. The creation of self-limitations by a sovereign power is no bar to their abolition by the same sovereign power. This is no argument for adopting a new constitution in a manner different from that provided in the instrument itself, for in the case of the constitution of this State, beyond the express statement of the right of the people to make and alter their constitution of government, the constitution is absolutely silent as to how this right may be carried into effect.

The contention herein made is that the majority have a right to make and alter their constitution of government, that this right cannot be abrogated, and that nothing to the contrary is to be found in our constitution, which does expressly reserve the right of the people to make and alter their form of government; and this, by necessary implication, carries with it the right of the general assembly to call a convention, when there is a recognized necessity for it; the right of such a convention to meet and frame a new constitution, that shall be submitted to the vote of the electors who will become qualified under its terms; and, lastly, the right of the majority to make such a new constitution, thus ratified by their votes, the supreme law of the state, subject, of course, to the constitution and laws thereunder of the United States. This and this only is a republican form of government in this land. The necessity for such a convention is everywhere acknowledged. Let the general assembly do its duty and call it.

The framers of our constitution, in omitting to provide how our people can make and alter their constitution of government, and in omitting to state that a majority can do it, it is logical to hold, must have meant, as the general assembly had already called four constitutional conventions, of which two had been called within two years of the convention that framed the present constitution, that the general assembly could call conventions again whenever necessity might demand. (See also Art. IV, Sec. 10.) They must also have meant that a majority can make and alter their constitution of government through the usual American channels and methods for bringing about such alterations and carrying them into effect. This includes the usual American rule that all this may be done by the majority. This natural presumption of conformity to established American usage is not rebutted by anything to be found in the constitution.

This is no proposal, therefore, to proceed in a manner differing from that laid down in the constitution, but is an argument to show that, the necessity being recognized, the general assembly should call a constitutional convention, that nothing in the constitution forbids or interferes with this course, and that it would be strictly in consonance with established American usage.

Logically the argument goes further and is—that no constitution limiting the power of the majority of the people to make and alter their constitution of government can prevent a majority of the people from doing so whenever necessity demands.

It so happens that in two states of the Union the constitution has been changed in a manner different from that provided in the previous constitution, i.e., Delaware, in 1791; and Maryland, in 1850. The defence offered for this course is most able and is entirely convincing. In 1858, Senator Bayard, of Delaware, father of the late senator, secretary of state and ambassador Bayard, contended in the senate of the United States that the people of Delaware had an inherent undefeasible right to change their constitution as a majority might deem wise. (See Appendix to Vol. 37, Cong. Globe, 1881.) He took the broad logical ground that a majority cannot be restrained, by restrictions in the constitution, from changing their fundamental law when and as they please. He held that the right to change is included in the right to organize, and that both can be exercised at any time by a majority. The right to organize is the right of the majority to govern and precludes any power in the majority that organizes to render the government unalterable except by more than a majority, "because such a restriction is inconsistent with their own power to form a government, and is at war with the very axioms from which their own power to act is derived." If a majority of the people has not the power to make a constitution binding forever or for a specific term of years, how can it have the power to make it binding forever unless changed by more than a majority? Whence can be derived the notion that a majority at any one time has more power than a majority at any other time?

Hon. Reverdy Johnson, United States senator from Maryland, wrote in part as follows, in 1864, concerning the action taken by the people of Maryland in changing their constitution in a different manner from that prescribed in the former constitution :

"No man denies that the American principle is well settled that all governments originate with the people and may, by like authority, be abolished or modified ; and that it is not within the power of the people, even for themselves, to surrender this right, much less to surrender it for those who are to succeed them."

A provision in any of the constitutions of the United States limiting the power of the majority to alter it would be simply void.

But it will be asked, if this be so, how can we give effect to Article XIII of our constitution providing for the adoption of amendments by a three-fifths vote only? Is not this a limitation upon the power of the people to make and alter their constitution of government?

It can only be defended upon the ground that it relates only to *amendments* and not to an entire change of the constitution; that the framers had this in mind when they drafted the instrument, and that it was intended to prevent the adoption by a majority only, when perhaps only a light vote might be cast, of an amendment or amendments not really coming from the people directly, but suggested or initiated only by their servant, the general assembly.

But this is rather an excuse for the clause than a defence of it. Indeed, on principle it cannot be defended. It is always a mistake to provide, directly or indirectly, that a constitution can not be rewritten by a majority and that an amendment can only be made a part of the constitution by more than a majority. The result will be that the party in power will play fast and loose with the power thus put into their hands, and will use the one method or the other according to their preference for or their opposition to the particular measure proposed. If they favor it, they will submit it to the vote of the electors in the way the easiest to carry it, that is, in the way requiring the least number of votes. If they oppose it, they will submit it in the way requiring the greatest number of votes to carry it into effect. Thus, under the guise of an amendment to the constitution, the party in power in this State not being particularly desirous that the measure should be adopted, has twice submitted to the electors of this State during the last year a revised constitution. It was an amendment to the existing constitution only as a legal fiction. In reality it was a new constitution as its title shows. Being submitted, however, as an amendment to the existing constitution, under the provisions of Art. XIII, it required a three-fifths vote, and this it failed to receive either time it was voted on. Strangely enough, this difference between the means of adopting a new constitution and an amendment to the constitution was exactly reversed in this "Revised Constitution" lately voted down. Article XIII, section 1 provides that amendments, after proposal by the votes of two-thirds of the members of both houses of two successive general assemblies, shall become a part of the constitution if approved by a majority of the electors voting thereon, while section 2 provides that no revision or amendment agreed upon by a constitutional convention shall take effect until submitted to and approved by three-fifths of those voting thereon. That is to say, the expressly reserved right in Article I, section 1, of the people "to make and alter their constitution of government" was to be so restricted that when ascertained through the act of the people by their delegates in convention assembled (the most direct and explicit expression of the sovereign will) it was to be allowed to go into effect only when approved by three-fifths of those voting thereon; but the will of the people's servant and agent, the general assembly, was to take effect when approved by a majority of those voting thereon!

The result of such a system would be that if the party in power wanted the particular change to become law they would carry it through as an amendment, even if it amounted to a series of amendments enough to make it a new constitution. But if they should not want the particular change or changes carried into effect it would be more easy to defeat it or them by the vote of a majority of adverse electors, upon its submission as a revision or amendment of the constitution under section 2 of Article XIII.

Constitutions are too sacred to be framed so that they can be juggled with in this way by a political machine. The obvious way to prevent this is to provide that revisions and amendments, whether through a constitutional convention or the initiative of the general assembly, shall become part of the constitution when approved by a majority of those voting thereon.

This is also in accord with the fundamental principle of all Anglo-Saxon government that the majority rules when its will is ascertained through the forms prescribed to this end. This is plainly what is meant by Washington in his language cited in and made a part of our constitution, Article I, section 1, " but that the constitution which at any time exists, till changed by an explicit and authentic act of the whole people, is sacredly obligatory upon all." When a majority of the electors voting thereon vote to approve a revision or an amendment of a constitution, submitted by a constitutional convention consisting of delegates duly elected, or submitted by a general assembly duly elected, this is a change by an explicit and authentic act of the whole people. And it is submitted, that while the people can limit the power of the general assembly to propose amendments by requiring a three-fifths, or two-thirds, or a unanimous vote, no limitation can be imposed upon the right of the people to themselves make and alter their constitution of government by their explicit and authentic act, and by the usual majority.

The only conceivable limitation would be one providing that no change in the constitution (whether amendment or revision) can be made unless the majority voting for it is a majority of all the electors. There is room for argument that it would be proper to exact the approval of such a majority in such an important political affair as a change in the fundamental law. But although possible, no State has yet made this requisite.

It will be urged, however, that provisions requiring a three-fifths majority, two-thirds majority, or other majority amounting to more than 50 per centum and one vote, are proper and desirable to prevent hasty action and ill-considered changes in the organic law. Such a claim involves a want of faith in the majority, inconsistent with faith in our American system of government. If government by the majority when the will of that majority is ascertained under the forms of law provided for that purpose is not to be relied upon, but needs such checks as these, then we might as well abandon our democratic form of government. Rather let us be consistent and thorough in our faith in that government, and in practice let us put our faith into full force and effect. Can it be that in England faith in such a government is more real and thorough-going than it is in the United States? For there, without even the safeguards of any written constitution as usually understood, the majority rules.

When we take into account these additional safeguards against ill-advised or hasty changes in the organic law, in our written constitutions, this hesitation about trusting the majority with full power over the making and altering their own constitutions of government is irrational, illogical, due to want of faith in our system of government, and should no longer be tolerated. In this State it is a relic of the policy of the adherents of the old charter to minimize so far as possible the adoption of a democratic form of government.

Although they put down Dorr, the fundamental principles he contended for were right, though some of his methods were wrong. His chief error was in appealing to arms. The force of an enlightened public opinion compelled the adoption of his principles, but still, while surrendering in the main, the land-owners, constituting the charter party, managed to prevent the complete adoption of the principle that the majority shall rule when their will is ascertained in a lawful, explicit, and authentic manner. It is time now, casting timidity aside, to adopt the principle in its entirety.

To deny it is necessarily to establish in its place an oligarchic form of government.

If a three-fifths or two-thirds majority is necessary to effect a change, then the power is in the minority of two-fifths or one-third to prevent it. This is inconsistent with the provision, Art. IV, Sec. 4, of the constitution of the United States, guaranteeing to every State in the Union a republican form of government: that state has not a republican form of government where two-fifths or one-third, and one, can prevent three-fifths or two-thirds less one, from making or altering their constitution of government. A republican form of government means a government in which the majority governs.

That our forefathers intended the majority should rule is evident from an examination of their compacts of government.

That of Providence of 1637 is:

"We. whose names are hereunder, desiring to inhabit in the town of Providence, do promise to subject ourselves, in active or passive obedience, to all such orders or agreements as shall be made for public good of the body, in an orderly way, *by the major assent* of the present inhabitants, masters of families, incorporated together into a town fellowship, and such others whom they shall admit unto them, only in civil things."
(1 R. I. Col. Recs. 14.)

That of Pocasset or Portsmouth :

"The 7th day of the first month, 1638.

We whose names are underwritten do here solemnly in the presence of Jehovah incorporate ourselves into a Bodie Politick and as he shall help, will submit our persons, lives and estates unto our Lord Jesus Christ, the King of Kings and Lord of Lords and to all those perfect and most absolute lawes of his given us in his holy word of truth, to be guided and judged thereby.—Exod. 24, 3-4. 2 Cron. 11, 3, 2 Kings 11, 17."

WILLIAM CODDINGTON (and 18 others).
(1 R. I. Col. Recs. 52.)

The second one at Portsmouth :

"Aprill the 30th 1639.

We, whose names are under [written doe acknowledge] ourselves the legall subjects of [his Majestie] King Charles, and in his name [doe hereby binde] ourzelves into a civill body politicke, unto his lawes according to matters of justice
WILL'M HUTCHINSON (and 28 others).

April 30. 1639

According to the true intent of the [foregoing instrument wee] whose names are above particularly [recorded, do agree] *Joyntly or by the major voice* to g [overne ourselves by the] ruler or Judge amongst us in all [transactions] for the space and tearme of one [yeare, —— he] behaving himselfe according to the t [enor of the same]."
(1 R. I. Col. Recs. 70.)

That of Newport (made before they moved from Pocasset).

"Pocasset. On the 28th of the 2d [month] 1639.
"It is agreed by us whose hands are underwritten, to propagate a Plantation in the midst of the Island or elsewhere : And doe engage ourselves to bear equall charges, answerable to our strength and estates in common : and that our determination shall be *by major voice* of Judge and elders : the Judge to have a double voice."
Present. WM. CODDINGTON, Judge (and eight others.)
(1 R. I. Col. Recs. 87.)

That upon the union of the island towns of Portsmouth and

Newport, being the General Court of Elections for Aquidneck, held at Portsmouth, 1641, for the two island towns :

"It is ordered and unanimously agreed upon that the Government which this Bodie Politick doth attend unto in this Island and the Jurisdiction thereof in favor of our Prince, is a DEMOCRACIE, or Popular Government, that is to say, it is in the Powre of the Body of Freemen orderly assembled *or the major part of them*, to make or constitute Just Lawes by which they will be regulated and to depute from among themselves such Ministers as shall see them faithfully executed between Man and Man."

(1 R. I. Col. Recs. 112.)

The charter of 1643–4 provides . . .

"Together with full Power and Authority to rule themselves and such others as shall hereafter inhabit within any Part of the said Tract of land by such a Form of Civil Government as by voluntary consent of all, *or the greater Part of them*, they shall find most suitable to their Estate and condition : and for that End to make and ordain such Civil Laws and Constitutions and to inflict such punishments upon Transgressors and for Execution thereof, so to place and displace Officers of Justice as they *or the greatest Part of them* shall by free Consent agree unto. Provideded nevertheless that the said Laws, Constitutions and Punishments for the Civil Government of the Said Plantations be conformable to the Laws of England, so far as the Nature and Constitution of the place will admit."

(1 R. I. Col. Recs. 143 at 145.)

The charter of 1663 provides that the inhabitants already planted and settled in the colony, and all who hereafter go to inhabit it, and all their children " shall have and enjoye all libertyes and immunities of ffree and natural subjects within any the dominions of vs, our heires or successors, to all intents constructions and purposes whatsoever, as if they and every of them, were borne within the realme of England."

(2 R. I. Col. Recs. 3 at 18.)

Among these " libertyes and immunities " is that of government by the majority.

At the session of the first general assembly at Portsmouth, 1647, the following was adopted :

"For the Province of Providence."

" It is agreed by this present Assembly thus incorporate, and by this present act declared, that the forme of Government established in *Providence Plantations* is DEMOCRATICALL, that is to say, a Government held by yᵉ free and voluntarie consent of all, or the greater parte of the free Inhabitants."

(1 R. I. Col. Recs. 156.)

(The portions in brackets are words worn away in the originals. The italics are ours.)

See, (p. 46), the charter granted to the town of Providence by the general assembly in 1648. And lastly, this right of the majority to rule is reserved in Article I, section 1, of the constitution now in force.

It will be seen from this survey that all the compacts of government ever framed in Rhode Island have provided for government by the majority, most of them in express words. The comparatively new doctrine that two-fifths can defeat the will of the majority has no foundation or support in the history of the State.

In Smith v. Nelson, 18 Vt. 511 at 550 (1846), it was decided that although voluntary associations make constitutions and pass by-laws that they declare are not to be altered except in a certain way or manner, as by the concurrence of two-thirds or at two different meetings, &c., "yet their constitution and by-laws may at any time be altered or abrogated by the same power which created them, and the vote of any subsequent meeting, abrogating or altering such constitution, though passed only by a majority, has as much efficacy as a previous vote establishing them. A constitution for a voluntary society may be proper, as an organization, but it has none of the powers or requisites of a constitution in political bodies, which emanates from a higher power than the legislature, and always is supposed to be enacted by a power superior to the legislative, and hence is unchangeable except by the body which established it; but that body can change it at pleasure"—by which is meant that the constitution cannot be changed by the legislature, but the people that made the constitution can likewise destroy it; and this implies the power to set aside by a majority a self-imposed limitation, such as that a change shall only be made by a three-fifths vote, or by a nine-tenths vote, or by a unanimous vote, or after ten years, or one hundred years, or, to suppose the most extreme case, that it never should be amended.

So the general assembly, by a majority vote, may adopt a rule that it shall pass laws only by a three-fifths vote. But the same majority that passes such a rule can at any time set it aside. Were the provision one fixed by a higher power, were it in the constitution of the State, the general assembly could not set it aside. But as a self-imposed limitation it is repealable by the same power that imposed it and by the same majority. So, if a clause in a State constitution declaring that any vote more than a majority is necessary to change the constitution, it would be a self-imposed limitation that could be set aside by the same power that imposed it, and that power is the majority of the electors as the representatives of the sovereign will. Were the provision one fixed by a higher power, were it in the constitution of the United States, it could only be set aside by the people of the United States in the mode provided for amending the constitution of the United States. It would no longer be a self-imposed limitation, subject to repeal by the same power that imposed it; it would be a limitation imposed by a higher power and subject to repeal only by that higher power.

Of course a sovereign body, so-called, can restrain itself. It does so constantly. Webster, in the celebrated case of Luther *v*. Borden, 7 How. R. 1, 6 Webster's Works, 217, said:

"But the people limit themselves also in other ways: * * * They limit themselves by all their constitutions in two important respects: that is to say, in regard to qualifications of *electors*, and in regard to the qualifications of the *elected*. In every state and in all the states the people have precluded themselves from voting for everybody they might wish to vote for; they have limited their own right of choosing. . . . They have also limited themselves to certain prescribed forms for the conduct of election."

But all these restrictions can be set aside by the same power that set them up. Wherein would a provision requiring more than a majority vote differ in this respect?

New Jersey set aside the law giving women the suffrage. New York adopted a new constitution in 1821 that excluded negroes from the suffrage they had hitherto enjoyed. Why cannot a provision requiring more than a majority vote be likewise set aside? There was no vested right to the suffrage that prevented taking it away from those to whom it had been granted by the vote of the majority. In the same way there would be no vested right to require more than a majority vote that would prevent the abolition of this provision by the vote of the same majority that established it.

No state in the Union has yet ordained, however, that the majority shall not make and alter their constitution of government. The nearest approach to it is the limitation· in Art. XIII of the constitution of this State, and this is distinguishable as only a limitation providing that more than a majority shall be requisite to adopt an amendment initiated by the general assembly and to be submitted to the electors only after it has been approved by a majority of all the members elected to the two houses of two successive general assemblies.

The commissioners who revised the constitution in 1897 took a strange fancy to this most undemocratic idea of limiting the will of the people, for they provided in Article XIII, section 2, that no revision or amendment of the revised constitution submitted by them, agreed upon by any constitutional convention, should take effect until submitted to the electors and approved by three-fifths of those voting thereon.

This is an attempt to deny the right of the people to recast their political institutions, whatever may be the necessity, and this, as Jameson on Const. Convs. 546, points out, cannot be done. This alone were reason enough for the rejection of the revised constitution. It is a bad policy to attempt by abstract rules of law to prevent great organic movements of the people acting through a majority of the electors. In case of conflict, something must give way, and it is hardly likely to be the majority. For the underlying principle of all English and American government is that the majority shall rule. It is not those who assert this principle that are asserting something revolutionary. It is those who deny it, who fear the rule of the majority, who would limit it, who assert that a presènt majority can deprive a future majority of the same power they enjoy, who assert that a majority for the time being can prevent a future majority to-morrow, next year, next century, throughout all the centuries to come, to the end of time, from making or altering their constitution of government that are asserting a revolutionary doctrine, unknown to the framers of all the compacts of governments of town and State ever framed in Rhode Island, and elsewhere, except to the framers of the restriction placed in the constitution of 1842 (Art. XIII) limiting the power to accept an amendment proposed by the general assembly, unless it receive three-fifths of the votes of the electors voting thereon, and the framers of the lately rejected "Revised Constitution." But time can confer no sanction on such a mischievous, undemocratic doctrine. That the so-called Law and Order party in 1842, afraid to trust the new electorate forced upon them against their will, put into the constitution a clause, the effect of which is supposed to be to destroy the expressly stated right of the people to make and alter their constitution of government by the usual majority vote, confers no greater authority or sanction upon such a revolutionary scheme now than it had then, and it clearly had none then. Yet, strange to say, fifteen able, educated men were found in this State who agreed to extend the scope and operation

3

of this dangerous and oligarchic principle. It is most extraordinary that fifteen representative men should have agreed on a proposition subversive of the very foundations of our political being.

Another excellent reason for the defeat of the revised constitution is found in the omission to impose new and necessary restraints upon the powers exercised by the general assembly.

It is well known to all who have studied the history of this State that the general assembly has always exercised enormous powers. This resulted from the great powers conferred upon this branch of the government under the charter granted by Charles II, in 1663, and the limited powers conferred upon the executive. The general assembly had judicial powers as well as legislative powers conferred upon it under this charter, and the dual nature of the general assembly continued until the constitution was adopted in 1842, and even then the exercise of judicial power by the general assembly was not given up until it was compelled to do so by the decision of our supreme court. (See Taylor v. Place, 4 R. I. 324.) This assumption of judicial power by the general assembly was of ancient growth, and its surrender, after the adoption of the constitution, was difficult.

The dread of centralized power was one of the principal motives that delayed until 1647 the adoption of the first or parliamentary charter, granted in 1643 by the committee of the long parliament, to the three original colonies of Providence, Portsmouth, and Newport. Warwick was admitted when this charter was accepted, although not named in it, this colony not being founded until 1642-3. These four original colonies or settlements, acquisitions in the east, and the region known as Narragansett constituted what is now the State of Rhode Island and Providence Plantations, and must not be confounded with the present towns or cities with the same names, the other towns of the State having been carved out from them, or erected in consequence of the settlements that grew up outside their limits.

May 4, 1776 this State passed its own declaration of independence, followed two months latter by the great Declaration of Independence.

This State continued until 1842 to govern itself under the forms of the royal charter, although without any formal sanction by the people. From May 4, 1776, to November 5, 1842, a period of more than sixty-six years, Rhode Island like England was under an unwritten constitution. As this is denied to be the fact by many, it is well to point out what those say who are competent to pass judgment upon it.

In Wilkinson *v.* Leland, 2 Peters 627 (1829), Story, J. said: "Rhode Island is the only State in the Union which has not a written constitution of government, containing its fundamental laws and institutions."

Jameson (on Const. Convs. 4th ed. 83) says: "Connecticut and Rhode Island had unwritten constitutions at the time of the Revolution, modelled in general after that of England, which continued in force until 1818 and 1842, respectively."

Cox, in his scholarly book on Judicial Power and Unconstitutional Legislation, 177, says: "It must here be recalled by the reader that the constitution of Rhode Island was, in 1786, an *unwritten* constitution, ascertained from history, not from the inspection of a written fundamental law denominated a constitution. Cf. Luther *v.* Borden, 7 How, 35, by Taney, C. J."

The point, although seemingly of thereoretical importance only, is very important in its bearings upon the "Dorr War" and its causes, when that incident is studied and its history is written by a competent hand.

The following year, 1787, the superior court of North Carolina, in Bayard *v.* Singleton (Martin's Reps. 1st Div. 48, 2d ed. 1, p. 42), held that the legislature could not pass a law the effect of which would be to alter the constitution of the State, without destroying the foundation of their own legislative authority.

This is what the general assembly of Rhode Island did when it severed the connection with the mother country May 4, 1776. It destroyed thereby the foundation of its own authority, and, as the act was and ever since has been accepted by the people, Rhode Island was thenceforth, until 1842, under an unwritten constitution.

We must accept this conclusion or hold that the act of May 4, 1776, was unconstitutional and void.

As Rhode Island, therefore, had no written constitution in the proper sense of that term, no constitution with a sanction, it was open to the people in 1842 to change their form of government as they pleased. It needed only that it should be the action of the majority and should become the government *de facto*. The appeal to arms by Dorr was a mistake. But after the suppression of this appeal to arms the general assembly granted what Dorr asked. A new constitution was framed, those who before were

excluded were allowed to take part in voting upon its adoption.
By their votes the demands of Dorr were accepted by a majority,
proving that the Dorrites were in a majority and that a political
mistake had been made in not granting their demands sooner.
Dorr's fame as a defender of the rights of the people was established, although not yet recognized as it should be. The time is
coming when Dorr will be looked upon as one of the greatest men
we have had.

In Rhode Island as in Connecticut the governor was not a crown
officer, and hence the revolution caused no break in the office of
the executive; and the provisions of the royal charter were liberal,
so that the general assembly exercising the powers conferred upon
it by the charter, and taking on new powers when necessity arose,
continued the government without difficulty until the "Dorr war"
in 1841. Had the party in power conceded at the outset what the
Dorrites asked for, this government might have continued indefi-
nitely.

The result of independence was to increase the powers, already
predominant, of our general assembly. One of the first checks
to this power was the decision in Trevett v. Weeden, in 1789, that
trial by jury being a part of the law of the land, an act of the
general assembly denying that right, in case of refusal to take
paper money for goods sold, was null and void. The case is of
great importance because it was the precursor of the since accepted doctrine that the judiciary can declare an act of the legislature unconstitutional when the question is involved in an actual
litigated case.

"The first reported American case in which a judicial judgment rejected a
legislative act as void because unconstitutional, was Trevett v. Weeden, which
arose in Rhode Island where the then constitution was not written."

(Cox. Judicial Power and Unconst. Legn. 177 and 160. See also Cooley, Const.
Limitations, 5th ed, 194, and the excellent report of this case in 1 Thayer, Cases
on Const. Law, 73.)

The fact that Rhode Island was governed under an unwritten
constitution made it easier for the court to take the position it
did, because it was not restrained by the fetters of a written constitution but could follow to their logical conclusions the intima-
tions in earlier English cases that led logically to the conclusion
they reached. See Cox's interesting examination of this important case.

Under the constitution adopted in 1842 the usual division into three coördinate branches, the legislative, the judicial, and the executive, was made. So firmly fixed in the minds of Rhode Islanders was the notion that the general assembly could do what it pleased, that it continued for years, notwithstanding the provisions of the constitution, to exercise judicial powers. It granted new trials of cases decided in the courts, heard and decided petitions for divorce, granted stays of judgment, etc.

In the celebrated case of Taylor v. Place, 4 R. I. 324, 1856, the supreme court put an end to this unconstitutional exercise of power by the general assembly. The decision in this case, by Ames, our greatest Rhode Island judge, should be studied by everyone who wants to understand the history of this State. To many the idea seemed preposterous that three men, elected to the bench by the general assembly, should dare to assert the unconstitutionality of an act by the general assembly that put them on that bench.

The cases of Trevett v. Weeden and Taylor v. Place, landmarks in the constitutional development of Rhode Island and the two most important cases in its political history, show emphatically the weak point in its government, the too great power of the general assembly. Any attempt to remodel the constitution must recognize this fact and remedy it. It renders it impossible to revise the constitution by proceeding under Article XIII to adopt a new constitution as an amendment to the existing one, because this requires the assent of a majority of all the members of each house of two successive general assemblies, and not even the usual majority of any one general assembly, nor of either house, can be expected to approve any measure, much less a radical revision, that will impose limitations upon the power of the general assembly. No organized body of men can be expected to take part in restricting its own powers, and our general assembly, with well established power, the result of the growth of power and the exercise thereof for two hundred and fifty years, is no exception to this rule. It is plain, therefore, that in order to place the necessary restrictions upon the power of the general assembly, recourse must be had to a constitutional convention. There is another excellent reason for this. A revised constitution adopted as an amendment to the existing constitution under Article XIII cannot be adopted except by the vote of three-fifths of those voting thereon. But if a constitutional convention be held under the exercise of the right of the people to make and alter their constitution of government expressly reserved in Article I, section 1, the new constitution submitted to the electors by such a convention would become the law of the land when approved by a majority of those voting thereon.

That a constitutional convention should be called, follows also from the well established principle (Jameson on Const. Conv. 211) "that whenever a constitution needs a general revision, a convention is indispensably necessary." That our constitution needs a general revision is attested by the well recognized consensus of public opinion and by the official declaration by the general assembly passed January 27, 1897, already cited, as follows:

" *Whereas*, there is a widespread feeling among the people of the State that the constitution should be carefully and thoroughly revised, and such changes as may seem to be advisable, in view of the changed condition of affairs since it was adopted, properly and carefully prepared."

There is still another reason why a convention should be called to revise the constitution. Safeguards are needed against the encroachments of a new danger, undreamt of by the framers of 1842—the power, unknown to the law, of the political machine under the control of unprincipled men, of the "boss" who controls them, and of those behind him. This new source of danger must be recognized and guarded against.

" We assume that we are living in a republic, a government of the people, by the people and for the people; a government in which responsibility follows privilege, or is that upon which privilege depends for existence, undivided responsibility, which no citizen can shirk or evade. Have we a wise, good, beneficent government, the people are happy. Is the government corrupt, the people suffer, but from their own folly. One of the most deplorable as well as dangerous tendencies of the age is the surrender of office-holding and the selection of holders of offices to professional office seekers and political rings. It is a question of doubt whether a government under the control of a boss or combination of bosses is republican. It is a serious question if the government of some of our States and many of our cities is not to-day an oligarchy. The necessity for the organization of the voters into parties, that certain distinctive and vital principles, upon which our people are divided, as their business or peculiar prejudices may necessitate, shall be made operative, furnishes the opportunity for the professional politician. Generally barren of principle, and with adjustable convictions, he is too often successful by the assistance of honest men, whose good nature and unsuspiciousness betray them into opening the gates, and the Greeks have entered Troy. The dictation of the boss forbids the consideration of the interests of the country, denies to the party he claims to represent the protection and conservation of its avowed principles, bends all the power of his personal machine to his own individual success and the rewarding of those whose influence and active coöperation he needs. Failure or neglect to placate the boss has tied the hands of the executive in city, State, and nation, blocking legislation and denying the representation of States in the congress of the nation. No longer is this tremendous power exercised in secret. The boss issues his fiat from the housetop, and the people, not realizing their danger, supinely yield. The undisguised purpose of the professional politicians, their source of power and cohesive force, is the desire for office and for office as a means of gain. How rarely does the question of ability or fitness to perform the responsible duties imposed enter into consideration when a candidate is to be selected for any position! Party loyalty, availability, pull, party service, is the shibboleth.—(*From I. A. Bassett's Memorial Day Address, May 30, 1899.*)

These are facts that cannot be ignored. They must be recognized, met, and overcome. To do this they must be discussed. To speak of them with bated breath, to tell privately how explanation of the necessity for a measure pending before the general assembly made to a member was met by the enquiry: "What does the old man think of it?" is not enough. If the price of liberty is eternal vigilance, we must be vigilant in guarding against new dangers as they arise. This new danger is a vital one; is common or becoming common in all the States of the Union, and can only be met by such new safeguards as nothing but a constitutional convention, with the after confirmation of the electors, can put into a new constitution.

It were folly for us in Rhode Island to deprecate the existence of a Platt or a Croker in New York, a Quay in Pennsylvania, a Gorman in Maryland, and so on through the whole infamous list, while ignoring the system of machine politics and boss rule in full operation in our own State. We must meet it and overcome it. We must amend our constitution to meet this new danger, and above all we must help to raise the sense of civic pride and municipal responsibility to a higher plane of political morality that will help to break up the infamous system.

In their advisory opinion of March 30, 1883, (14 R. I. at p. 654) the judges erred in saying that any new constitution which a convention could form would be a new constitution only in name. This proceeds upon the assumption that the bill of rights is a finished product, and that nothing can be added to it. But the bill of rights did not spring into being at one stroke. It was the result of centuries of effort to right centuries of wrongs. It represents the results of the conflict of ages between the powers that make for good and the powers that make for evil. As to each right secured there was a time when a wrong existed without legal remedy to prevent it. Each victory for the right became a new clause in the bill of rights.

No greater mistake could be made than to suppose that this conflict is ended and the bill of rights is finished. The year before the habeas corpus act was passed it might equally well have been claimed that the bill of rights contained "the great historic safeguards of liberty and property," and yet the next year added one of its most important provisions. It is not thus that liberty won is to be preserved, nor must we think the contest is ended. In the conflict between two rival powers, no state of permanent equilibrium can be long maintained. Ever watchful, the powers that make for evil, repressed in one direction, seek new directions, manifest themselves in new forms and must be met in their new forms, if our rights to liberty and property are to be maintained. Machine politics and boss rule are the present new forms of the powers that work for evil, and must be met, fought, and overcome. The victory will be recorded as a new clause in the bill of rights, as former victories were thus recorded. The people that rests serenely upon its old guaranties to liberty and property, without meeting and overcoming the new forms of assault thereon, will soon begin to lose what their more sturdy forefathers painfully acquired.

It is therefore impossible to make the changes that have become necessary in our constitution, whether they be called amendments, or a revised constitution, or a new constitution, except through a constitutional convention, for the reasons already set forth, and that may be summed up in one general characterization : the necessity for restrictions upon the powers of the general assembly and augmentation of the powers of the executive and judiciary.

The difference between the right of the people to make and alter their constitution of government under Article I, section 1, and the right of the general assembly to initiate amendments that shall become operative only when sanctioned by the people according to the peculiar and unusual terms of Article XIII, goes, therefore, to the very root of the matter, and is not matter of form but of very substance. To ignore it, as the advisory opinion does, is but to contribute to the political subjugation of the people, to the exaltation of the general assembly, the agent of the people, and to the making them the master instead of the servant.

It is notorious to students of contemporaneous American political history that the political machines in many of our States have seized with avidity upon a new device for securing political plums for their followers. Claiming that towns and cities are creatures of the State and may be controlled or even annihilated by the State, they claim, further, that the State may appoint officers to perform certain duties in the towns and cities, to be paid such salaries as the State may dictate, although the town or city is to have no control over these officers and protests against their appointment. In too many of the States the courts have maintained the legality of this course, sometimes through ignorance of their own political history and constitutional development, sometimes because the State is a new one, never had such a history and constitutional development as did the New England States and a few others, and, therefore, the ground put forward for such action has a better foundation. But we shall find in many of the cases denying the correctness of this theory, that the members of the court giving opinions adverse to the right of the State to appoint these officers, see plainly to what cause is due the theory that is set up that the State has the right to appoint these town and city officers, and they see that the allowance of the theory will result in the political enslavement of the towns and cities in this particular. See, for instance, People *v.* Hurlbut, 24 Mch. 44; State *v.* Moores, 76 N. W. Rep. 175; People *v.* Albertson, 55 N. Y. 50; State *v.* Denney, 118 Ind. 382 and many other authorities therein cited. 1 Bryce Am. Com. 611, 612. Report of Fassett Committee, 1891, 5 N. Y. Sen. Com. Rep. 459. At p. 13 this committee reports, speaking of the conditions existing and the assumption of power over towns and cities by the legislatures: "that local self government is a misnomer, and that consequently so little interest is felt in matters of local business, that in almost every city in the State it has fallen into the hands of professional politicians." Here we find the fertile source of loss of civic pride and the political decadence of American cities. They are admitted to be the worst governed of all the civilized countries of the world. We can only improve them by incorporating in the constitution recognition of the right of all towns and cities to self-government in their own affairs, and this can only be done through a constitutional convention.

This brings us to the reasons why the commission appointed under authority of the resolution of 1897 submitted a revised constitution that failed to meet the approval of the people. It did not contain the necessary restrictions upon the powers of the general assembly. This was not the fault of the excellent commission, but of the limitations imposed upon it in the very nature of the case. The commissioners well knew that the general assembly has too much power, and that new restrictions were needed upon its exercise. They were specifically pointed out to them, and drafts of clauses were submitted to them that would accomplish the end desired. But they also well knew that their work must receive the approval of a majority of all the members elected to each house of two successive general assemblies before the electors could vote on it. They knew that it would be impossible to secure such approval if they placed these necessary restrictions upon the powers of the general assembly in it, and hence they omitted them. The result was a revised constitution that was satisfactory to the general assembly, but was not satisfactory to the people of the State. No new constitution will be satisfactory to them that does not embody these necessary restrictions upon the power of the general assembly. A constitutional convention composed of delegates elected by the people can alone do this, and their work can only be made the law of the land when it shall be submitted to the people and accepted by the vote of the majority of the electors, these electors to include those who will become electors under the new constitution. Such has been the course pursued in the past, and there is no reason the same course should not be followed again.

It will be claimed that it has been decided, whether rightly or wrongly it matters not, by the judges of the supreme court, that the general assembly has no power to call a constitutional convention, and there is nothing to be done but to accept this decision and give up all attempts to procure a convention.

This would be to ignore the thoroughly well recognized distinction between an advisory opinion of the judges and an actual decision by the court in a litigated case. This is the common device of those who, not wanting a constitutional convention, shelter themselves behind this false shield. Having such profound deference for the court, why do they not also defer to the court's own repeated declaration and recognition of the distinction pointed out?

In Taylor *v.* Place, 4 R. I. 324 (1856), the same question came before the supreme court in a litigated case that the justices had previously given an advisory-opinion upon to the governor. The court said :

" This is the first time since the adoption of the constitution that this question has been brought judicially to the attention of the court. The advice or opinion given by the judges of this court, when requested, to the governor, or to either house of the general assembly, under the third section of the tenth article of the constitution, is not a *decision* of this court; and, given as it must be, without the aid which the court derives in adversary cases from able and experienced counsel, though it may afford much light from the reasonings or research displayed in it, can have no weight as a precedent." (By Ames, C. J., at p. 362.)

Upon the petition of W. Knowles for an opinion of the court, under Pub. Laws Ch. 563, sec. 6, April 20, 1876 (in 13 R. I. 9, July 3, 1880), the supreme court of this State gave an advisory opinion, only the petitioners being represented by counsel. The court afterwards had the same subject before them again, in an actual case, and, after a full hearing and argument on both sides, they reversed their former opinion, giving as one of their reasons for doing so, the fact that the first case, above cited "was a petition for an opinion on a case stated, and was doubtless submitted without full argument or presentation of authorities * * * * But we have no doubt that we should have decided the case differently if we had had before us, when we decided it, the same array of authorities which we have before us now." (See Allen *vs.* Danielson, 15 R. I. 480 at 482, March 5, 1887.)

The supreme court of this State has therefore decided twice that its own advisory opinion is not conclusive when the same matter comes before the court as an actual contested case.

This distinction has been recognized in many other courts and is admitted by all lawyers. Thus Kent, J., in 58 Me. 573, said :

" It is true, unquestionably, that the opinions given under a requisition of any officer, or any department, have never been regarded as binding upon the body asking for them."

Tapley, J., in 58 Me. 615, said :

" We can only proceed in the investigation upon the views of the law appertaining to the question as they appear to us upon first presentation, and anticipate as well as we can the ground which may be urged for or against the proposition presented, never regarding the opinions thus formed as conclusive, but open to review upon every proper occasion."

In 72 Me. 542 at 562, Libbey, J., said, Walton, J., concurring:

"Inasmuch as any opinion now given can have no effect if the matter should be judicially brought before the court by the proper process, and lest, in declining to answer, I may omit the performance of a constitutional duty, I will very briefly express my opinion upon the question submitted."

English authority is to the same effect, and is of weight, because it is from the English custom we have borrowed the system of asking the judges for their advice upon questions of law. Thus, for centuries, the king called upon the judges of England for their opinions. The answers of the judges to such questions are not and never have been looked upon as opinions in the sense of being judicial determinations that are binding and final, but as advisory opinions only, entitled to respect as opinions of men learned in the law, but as nothing more. Thus McQueen on the Appellate Jurisdiction of the House of Lords, p. 39, says:

"It has been sometimes asked whether the opinions of the judges ought not to govern the decision of the house. They have never had that effect, even when unanimous, and it is not easy to see how they could so operate when conflicting and opposed. The house pays great regard to the opinions of the judges, especially when concurrent. But the house cannot transfer to others the constitutional responsibility which attaches to the adjudication of causes in the court of last resort. The opinions of the judges, however, even though not adopted by the house, must always be expected to throw valuable light on the subject of its deliberations."

Many other authorities to the same effect may be found in the able articles on "The Duty of Judges as Constitutional Advisers," by H. A. Dubuque, Esq., in 24 Am. Law Rev. 369, and by Prof. Thayer of the Harvard Law School, "On the Origin and Scope of the American Doctrines of Constitutional Law," in 7 Harv. Law Rev. 153.

In one case the advisory opinion of the judges of a State supreme court on a question of law (8 Mass. 549) has been reversed in an actual case, involving the same question, by the decision of the highest court of the land, the supreme court of the United States (12 Wheat. 19). It has never been contended nor decided that an advisory opinion is *res judicata*, and therefore binding, and is beyond change or reversal, or that an act of the general assembly contrary to the advisory opinion of the judges would be unconstitutional. It is time this specious and flimsy excuse for not doing what the general assembly has decided to be necessary, were swept away. For by its resolution passed January 27, 1897, already cited, the general assembly has declared that the constitution should be thoroughly revised. The only way now left to accomplish this is through a constitutional convention. The general assembly should therefore pass an act at once, calling a constitutional convention, the result of whose labors should be submitted to the people, meaning thereby, of course, the vote of the electors, the representatives of the people in such a case.

If the general assembly, lacking the courage to act, or doubting its own power, still hesitates, it should submit the question again to the judges with an opportunity, such as the judges themselves said they would be glad to have, to give more careful study to the subject, with an opportunity for the presentation of all views relating thereto, with full argument thereon and presentation of authorities, in order that the conclusions reached may merit the confidence, approval, and support of the people of the State.

Should the general assembly deem either of these courses inadvisable, then it should submit to the electors, under the provisions of Article XIII of the constitution, an amendment to the constitution providing for the calling of a constitutional convention, which call should provide that the new constitution prepared by the convention shall go into effect if approved by a majority of the electors voting thereon, such electors to include those who will become electors under the provisions of such new constitution.

But we shall be reminded of the maxim : " *Expressio unius est exclusio alterius,*" cited by the judges in their opinion, as decisive on this point.

" I may observe that the method of construction summarized in the maxim ' *expressio unius exclusio alterius* ' is one that certainly requires to be watched. Perhaps few so-called rules of interpretation have been more frequently misapplied and stretched beyond their due limit."
(By Willis, J., in Colquhon *v.* Brooks, 57 L. J. Q. B. 70.)

" It is often a valuable servant but a dangerous master to follow in the construction of statutes or documents. The *exclusio* is often the result of inadvertence or accident, and the maxim ought not to be applied when its application, having regard to the subject matter to which it is to be applied, leads to inconsistency or injustice."
(By Lopes L. J., in Colquhon *v.* Brooks, 57 L. J. Q. B. 439.)

An express limitation upon the power of the general assembly to propose amendments to the constitution (Art. XIII) is not, and cannot by any logical construction, be construed into an implied limitation upon the power of the people to meet in convention, by delegates elected for that purpose, to make and alter their constitution of government. (Art. I. Sec. 1.) These are two different things, and a construction is to be favored that will give effect to both articles. This is no party question, but purely one of constitutional law, nor is any one proposing anything contrary to the constitution, but to give effect to the whole of the constitution. Blackstone *381, citing Cro. Eliz. 420, and 1 Vern. 30. This the advisory opinion of the judges failed to do, and to this extent the advisory opinion of the judges, failing, as it does, to give effect to both clauses of the constitution, proposes something not in accord with the constitution, and is, therefore, itself unconstitutional.

A legislative construction had been placed upon this subject by these frequent calls for a convention issued by the general assembly. The question is a political one rather than a legal one, and therefore on both these grounds the judges might well have declined to express their opinion on it.

Our forefathers would have been astonished indeed had it been foretold to them that by an implied construction, quasi-judicial only, of the section relating to amendments initiated by the general assembly their successors were to be deprived of the expressly stated right to make and alter their constitution of government.

In their advisory opinion the judges converted an express grant of authority to an agent, i. e., the general assembly, to initiate amendments, in one article of the constitution, into an implied restraint upon the expressly stated right of another party in another article to do a different thing, i. e., to make and alter their constitution of government, thus setting up a new and unheard of rule of construction.

There is but one proper application of the maxim in the case of our constitution, i.e., the expressly mentioned way in Article XIII of the manner in which the general assembly may propose amendments is an exclusion of any other way in which they can propose them. To that extent the application of the maxim " *Expressio unius est exclusio alterius* " is sound. It is denied, however, that framing a new constitution by a convention is amending the existing constitution. To use a homely illustration, the man who re-shingles his house repairs it, but he who pulls his old house to pieces and builds a new one, though he uses the beams and planks that were in the old house to build his new one with, adding such new material as may be necessary, does not repair it—he builds a new house.

The exercise by the people through a constitutional convention of their power to make and alter their constitution of government under Article I, section 1, is an entirely different thing from the exercise of the power of the general assembly to propose amendments to the constitution only in the expressly limited way set forth under Article XIII.

But what the members of the court held, in effect, in their advisory opinion, was that express power given to one party, (the general assembly, the agent) to do a certain thing (to propose amendments) in an expressly limited way (through action by a special majority of two successive general assemblies, their proposals to go into effect only when approved by a special majority of the electors) is an implied limitation upon the expressly stated power of another party (the people, the principal) to do another thing (to make and alter their constitution of government) in another way (by a constitutional convention). It would be difficult to conceive of circumstances under which the application of the maxim could be more misplaced.

Instead of applying the maxim in such a way as to exclude the possibility of a constitutional convention (by giving exclusive effect to Art. XIII and none to Art. I, Sec. 1) it would be more consonant with broad sound principles of construction to apply the maxim, under Art. I, Sec. 1, as reserving the absolute right of the people to make and alter their constitution of government, and as excluding any restriction thereon under Art. XIII. The expression of the right of the people to make and alter their constitution of government, the *expressio unius*, is exclusive; and, therefore, it is the *exclusio* of any other mode, leaving to the general assembly the ordinary legislative power to call upon the people to meet in convention when necessity demands.

But the maxim has no real application, because Art XIII relates to a different thing. It merely provides a method by which the agent, the general assembly, may initiate amendments—by providing a special majority of two successive general assemblies instead of the usual majority of one general assembly, and a special majority of the electors to carry the initiative of the general assembly into effect, instead of the usual majority. The maxim does not apply, because the *expressio unius* is not the same in the two articles. As Jameson says (p. 605, 4th ed. Const. Convs.), the maxim does not apply, "because the people could not do *the same thing* in a different way, it does not follow that they could not do a *different* thing in a *different* way." Therefore a limitation upon the power of one party to do one thing in one way is no limitation upon the power of another party to do another thing in another way. Especially is this true when it is possible to adopt a construction that will give full force and effect to both provisions of the constitution. The objection to the construction adopted by the judges is that it finds an implied limitation in Art. XIII, therefore Art. XIII is exclusive of all other methods, and hence denies all effect to the expressly stated power of the people to make and alter their constitution of government, under Art. I, Sec. 1. It is not thus constitutional guarantees are to be construed.

Contending that the general assembly has come to exercise too much power and that a constitution drawn to suit the wants of the present time should limit that power, it becomes necessary to review the constitution of the State, to show what the original powers of the four towns constituting the colony were, what they were in the towns admitted after the charter was accepted, how they have been gradually curtailed by the general assembly, what remain to them now and should be preserved specifically in a new constitution.

In People *v.* Harding, 53 Mich. 485 (1884), Cooley, C. J., said:

"In seeing for the real meaning of the constitution we must take into consideration the times and circumstances under which the State constitution was formed, the general spirit of the times and the prevailing sentiments among the people. Every constitution has a history of its own which is more or less peculiar; and unless interpreted in the light of this history, is liable to be made to express purposes which were never within the minds of the people in agreeing to it."

No constitution is wholly written, even in this, the home of the written constitution. For instance, the power of the judiciary to declare a law unconstitutional and therefore void, when the question comes before them in an actual, litigated case, America's most valuable contribution to political government is not expressly stated in any written constitution. It is, however, as much a part of the common law of the land, as a part of the unwritten constitution, as if it were expressly stated in the written constitution. Rhode Island contributed largely to this new check upon the power of the legislature by the action taken by its supreme court in 1789, in the celebrated case of Trevett *v.* Weeden, already considered.

Perhaps the fact that Rhode Island was governed under an unwritten constitution from May 4, 1776, when it declared its independence of England, to November 5, 1842, when the present constitution was signed, made it easier for the judiciary to assume this power. It certainly made it easier for the general assembly, the most powerful branch of the government, to assume new powers from time to time thereafter.

Nor is any constitution wholly unwritten. The Bill of Rights, the Act of Settlement concerning the succession to the throne, the oaths of office taken by the king and the members of parliament, even Magna Charta itself, being in the nature of compacts entered into by different parties, are formal sanctions of so much of the organic or fundamental law of England as parts of a written constitution, and theoretically, at least, they can be abrogated only by the consent of both parties thereto. The difficulty is that there is no means provided in England whereby a violation thereof can be declared null and void. Should the king violate these parts of a written constitution, he may be impeached; but should parliament violate them, there is no remedy.

In People *v.* Hurlbut, 24 Mich. 44 (1871), at p. 107, Cooley J. said:

"If this charter of State government which we call a constitution were all there was of constitutional command; if the usages, the customs, the maxims that have sprung from the habits of life, modes of thought, methods of trying facts by the neighborhood and mutual responsibility in neighborhood interests; the precepts that have come to us from the revolutions which overturned tyrannies; the sentiments of manly independence and self-control which impelled our ancestors to summon the local community to redress local evils, instead of relying upon king or legislature at a distance to do so—if a recognition of all these were to be stricken from the body of our constitutional law, a lifeless skeleton might remain, but the living spirit, that which gives it force and attraction, which makes it valuable, and draws to it the affections of the people; that which distinguishes it from the numberless constitutions, so-called, which in Europe have been set up and thrown down within the last hundred years, many of which, in their expressions, seemed equally fair and to possess equal promise with ours, and have only been wanting in the support and vitality which these alone can give—this living and breathing spirit which supplies the interpretation of the words of the written charter, would be utterly lost and gone."

The ninth article of Magna Charta provides:

5

" The City of London shall have all the old liberties and customs which it hath been used to have. Moreover we will and grant that all other Cities, Boroughs, Towns, and the Barons of the Five Ports and all other Ports, shall have all their liberties and free customs."

One of the most cherished of these liberties was the right of local self-government: can it be contended that this right is lost because not expressly reserved in the written constitution? Is it not a part of the unwritten constitution, one of the common law rights brought over from England by our ancestors, and never surrendered?

It must be remembered also that our form of government is not one in which all power is in the legislative, judicial, and executive branches thereof unless expressly reserved to the people. On the contrary, all power remains in the people that is not expressly delegated to one of the three branches named. See, State *v.* Denny, 118 Ind. 449 (1888), by Olds, J., at p. 457.

A constitution " grants no right to the people, but is the creature of their power, the instrument of their convenience * * * *. A written constitution is in every instance a limitation upon the powers of government in the hands of agents."

(Cooley Const. Lims., 5th ed. 47.)

In Rhode Island the four original towns were really separate colonies, and existed before there was any Rhode Island. They made it by their union. Providence was settled in 1636; Portsmouth, originally Pocasset, in 1638; Newport, in 1639; and Warwick, in 1642–3. These were the original colonies, or towns, of this State. They must not be confounded with the present towns of the same names, but it must be remembered that many of the later towns have been carved out of these four original colonies and have the same rights, duties, and powers that the original colonies, or towns, had. Each one of these first three had its own agreement of association, voluntarily entered into without sanction of any kind from crown or parliament, sufficient to enable its inhabitants to maintain its separate political existence, and each one acquired the title to its lands by purchase from the Indians. The first of these written compacts that has come down to us is that of Providence, signed in 1636 by thirteen of the founders. It is the most famous, for its setting forth, but only negatively and by implication, of Roger Williams' contribution to political government, the doctrine of the utter separation of State and church that became distinctively Rhode Island doctrine and thence spread to every State in the Union, and is now spreading to every civilized land. This compact, here again cited, was as follows:

" We whose names are hereunder, desirous to inhabit in the town of Providence, do promise to subject ourselves in active or passive obedience to all such orders or agreements as shall be made for public good of the body, in an orderly way, by the major assent of the present inhabitants, masters of families, incorporated together into a town fellowship, and such others whom they shall admit unto them, only in civil things."
(1 R. I. Col. Recs. 14.)

The original may still be seen in the city hall, Providence, framed and hung between two plates of glass.

From the momentous consequences that have resulted from it, it is certainly one of the most famous compacts of government in existence.

The first compacts of government, in Portsmouth, in Newport, and in the first union, that of the island towns, have already been cited.

The settlers at Warwick did not form any corporation or agreement of association of any kind, claiming that as English subjects they had no right to erect a government without authority from the crown or government in England. They continued without any government and officers until the charter of 1643 was accepted and an organization thereunder perfected in 1647.

Warwick was not named in the charter of 1643, because it was only settled the year the charter was granted. No acceptance of the charter and union under it took place until 1647, and then Warwick was admitted on the same footing as the other colonies, the record simply stating :   •

"It was agreed that Warwick should have the same privileges as Providence.".
(1 R. I. Col. Recs. 148.)

It would seem that traces of the influences resulting from the union of the island towns (p. 38) were here manifest—that Providence was admitted to join them "in the modell that hath been latelie shewn vnto us by our worthy Friends of the island," thus recognizing the fact that the two island towns were already united and now Providence was to be allowed to come in also. The record in full is as follows:

" 6. It was ordered, upon the request of the Commissioners of the Towne of Providence, that their second instruction should be granted and established unto

them, Vidg't. Wee do voluntarily assent, and are freely willing to receive and to be governed by the Lawes of England, together with the way of the Administration of them, soe far as the nature and constitution of this Plantation will admit, desiring (soe far as possible may be) to hold a correspondence with the whole Colonie in the modell that hath been latelie shewn vnto us by our worthy Friends of the island, if the Generall Courte shall compleat and confirm the same, or any other modell as the General Courte shall agree vpon according to our Charter.'
(1 R. I. Col. Recs. 147.)

We have, therefore, the settlement of Providence, Portsmouth, and Newport, before any charter whatsoever from England, the settlement of Warwick the same year the charter was granted, the purchase from the Indians, and the adoption of self-formed compacts of government independently of the mother country or of any charters granted in England, and the exercise of the necessary powers of government.

The settlement at Portsmouth, in 1638, was made at the upper end of the island of Aquidneck; that at Newport, in 1639, at the lower end of the island by a minority of the principal settlers at Portsmouth. They carried with them the records made to that time and continued them at Newport.

The separate colonies exercised such judicial powers as were necessary for their peace and safety. The first instance we find was in 1637, when Joshua Verin was tried in town-meeting, convicted, and disfranchised for not allowing his wife to hear Roger Williams preach, as she wanted to. This was done by the major assent of the freemen in open town-meeting.

"It was agreed that Joshua Verin, upon the breach of a covenant for restraining of the libertie of conscience, shall be withheld from the libertie of voting till he shall declare the contrary." (1 R. I. Col. Recs. 16).

In 1637 a new and more elaborate form of government was adopted, with provisions for settlement of disputes between the townsmen by arbitration. (1 R. I. Col. Recs. 27.)

Foster (Town Government in Rhode Island, 18) says:

"There are some minor variations between the practice of Providence and that of Portsmouth. For instance, in the former town the administration of justice was committed to the whole body of citizens, with at first absolutely no discrimination. The next step was to select two 'deputies.' In Portsmouth, on the other hand, the citizens began by choosing one of their number 'Judge.'"

"The 7th of the first month, 1638.
We that are Freeman Incorporate of this Bodie Politick, do Elect and Constitute William Coddington Esquire, a Judge amongst us, and so covenant to

yield all due honour unto him according to the lawes of God, and in so far as in us lyes to maintaine the honour and privileges of his place which shall hereafter be ratified according unto God, the Lord helping us so to do.

WILLIAM ASPINWALL, *Sec'y."*

(1 R. I. Col. Recs. 52.)

Later, in the same year, three "elders were associated with him "in the Execution of Justice and Judgment." (1 R. I. Col. Recs. 63.) Yet even they were obliged to make a quarterly account of their rulings to the town-meeting (in early records designated "the Bodey.")

In September, 1638, the Portsmouth town-meeting summoned eight inhabitants whom it tried, convicted and sentenced, some for drunkenness, some for rioting. (1 R. I. Col. Recs. 60.)

In another instance the Portsmouth town-meeting condemned and divided the property of an absconding debtor (do. 64.)

April 30, 1639, after the minority had left, to found Newport, a new organization was perfected and signed by twenty-nine persons. (1 R. I. Col. Recs. 70.) An act was passed the same day appointing seven assistants a court for settling disputes involving less than forty shillings. Provision was also made for a quarterly court of trials with a jury of twelve men.

Oct. 1, 1639:

"It is ordered that every Tuesday in the Month of July, the Judge and Elders shall assemble together to heare and determine all such causes as shall be presented."

(1 R. I. Col. Recs 90.)

This would seem to have been in the nature of a court of appeal. On the same page may be found the record showing that in the quarterly town-meetings, called the quarter courts, "the determination of the matters in hand shall be by major vote, the judge having his double vote who also shall have power to putt it to vote and to gather up the votes."

The judge was becoming the chief executive officer.

Arnold, p. 138, calls attention to the fact that the due administration of justice very early occupied the attention of these colonists. He says:

"A formal act of the whole people, passed at this time will set their regard for justice, and their care in providing for its administration, in still clearer light:

'By the Body Politicke in the Ile of Aqethnec, Inhabiting this present, 25 of 9: month 1639.

In the fourteenth yeare of ye Raigne of our Soveraigne Lord King Charles. It is Agreed. that as Natural Sublects to our Prince, and subject to his Lawes, All matters that concerne the Peace shall bee by those that are Officers of the Peace. Transacted : And All actions of the Case or Debt shall bee by such Courts as by Order are Here appointed, and by such Judges as are Deputed : Heard and Legally Determined. Given at Nieu-port on the Quarter Day Courte Day which was adjourned until ye Day. WILLIAM DYRE, Sec."'

This colony, therefore, established a judicial system of its own, civil and criminal, the year it was founded, four years before any application was made for a charter and eight years before organization under the charter granted. Evidently the courts of this town did not derive their powers and jurisdiction from the general assembly nor from any authority across the sea.

In 1640 a union was brought about between the two colonies on the island of Aquidneck, Portsmouth and Newport.

"It is ordered, that the Chiefe Magistrate of the Island shall be called Governour, and the next Deputie Governor, and the Rest of the Magestrates Assistants ; and this to stand for a decree."

"It is agreed that the Govenor and two Assistants shall be chosen in one Town, and the Deputy Govenour and two other Assistants in the other Town." (1 R. I. Col. Recs. 100.)

It will be seen that the towns were not fused into one town, but that 'each kept up its own existence, forming a union for their common objects, but leaving to each its own local affairs. This has always been the leading characteristic of American union, wherever found. The governour and assistants (now senators) were invested with the offices of the justices of the peace, this being the beginning of a centralized judicial authority. The "particular courts," consisting of magistrates and jurors, were ordered to be held monthly in each town. These courts had jurisdiction in cases in the respective towns, not involving life and limb. There was a right of appeal to the quarter sessions, (1 R. I. Col. Recs. 113), and two annual parliamentary or generall courts were provided, " equally to be kept at the two towns (1 R. I. Col. Recs. 106). The laws were revised. The majority of the freemen of each town were empowered to select men from themselves to lay forth each man's land and to record their doings. The land titles have been so recorded in each town ever since. Provision was made for each town to have a joint and an equal supply of money in the treasury, to be drawn by warrant according to the determination of the major vote of the towns, respectively, each town to bear its proportion of the joint expense. (1 Col. Recs. 106.) The assessment and collection of the tax was left to each town, and there it has ever remained in Rhode Island. (Gen. Laws R. I. cap. 36, sec. 3 and ch. 29.)

"It is ordered, that each Towne shall have the Transaction of the affaires that shall fall within their own Towne." (1 R. I. Col. Recs. 106.)

And such has ever been the custom in Rhode Island, although no such express statement can be found in the written constitution. The time has come now, in view of the encroachments made by the general assembly upon this right of our towns to local self-government, that it should be put in the constitution in order that further encroachments may be stopped.

In 1641 an explicit statement was made as to the form of government of this union.

"It is ordered and unanimously agreed upon that the Government which this Bodie Politicke doth attend vnto in this Island, and the Jurisdiction thereof, in favour of our Prince, is a DEMOCRACIE, or Popular Government : that is to say, It is in the Powre of the Body of Freemen orderly assembled, or the major part of them, to make or constitute Just Lawes, by which they will be regulated, and to depute from among themselves such Ministers as shall see them faithfully executed between Man and Man."

"It was further ordered, by the authority of this Present Courte, that none bee accounted a Delinquent for *Doctrine:* Provided it be not directly repugnant to ye Government or Lawes established." (1 R. I. Col. Recs. 112.)

"It was also ordered that a Manual Seale shall be provided for the State, and that the Signett or Engraving thereof, shall be a sheafe of Arrows bound up, and in the Liess or Bond, this motto indented : *Amor vincet omnia.*" (1 R. I. Col. Recs. 115.)

This is cited because here we find used for the first time the word "State."

"The possession of a seal has always been held as one of the insignia of sovereignty or of exclusive rights. Its adoption by a yet unchartered government was significant."
(1 Arnold, Hist. R. I. 149.)

Here, in 1641, three years before a charter was applied for and six years before the one granted was accepted, we find two independent colonies each reserving its right to local self-government, including its own court, uniting to form a State; adopting a seal and establishing a government for the whole body, consisting of a legislature, a judiciary, and an executive. The significance of this movement has never been adequately recognized. No power, either of the two individual colonies nor of the united colony, was derived from the crown, parliament, nor from any charter. We see, also, that before the grant of the first charter, two of the towns, setting up a joint government of their own, exercised these rights of sovereignty. Hence they did not receive these rights from the colony or State, but, rather, conferred rights upon the colony or State that they created by their union.

One of the most important acts passed was the one, above cited, establishing religious liberty, already established in Providence.

"The people, having recently transferred the judicial power from their own control to the courts and juries, they enacted this law, protecting liberty of conscience, not choosing to trust the judiciary with the keeping of that sacred principle for which they had transported themselves, first from England, and then from Massachusetts. It was the foundation of the future Statutes and Bill of Rights, which distinguished the early laws and character of the State and people of Rhode Island from the other English colonies in America."

(Bull, Memoir of Rhode Island.)

The details of the proceedings of this first general assembly of the two united colonies may be followed: pages 124 to 162 of Arnold's History of Rhode Island.

The general assembly in 1643-44, changed the name of the island from Aquidneck to "The Isle of Rhodes or Rhode Island," by which name it has since been known. The dual name of "The State of Rhode Island and Providence Plantations" arose from the union of the Aquidneck government with that of Providence, under the charter of 1663.

The general officers elected in 1641 continued in office until the charter government was organized in 1647. The records of the general court of this union cease in 1644, and the town records of Newport are lacking. The mutilated pages of the Portsmouth town records help to fill the gap and confirm the fact that if no general court was convened in this interval, town-meetings were held in both towns and their decrees were duly executed.

The data given show that Providence, Portsmouth, Newport, and Warwick existed as separate colonies until they united. The colony of Rhode Island was formed by their union. They were the precursors or forefathers of the colony, and the colony was their offspring. When Channing in his " United States of America " (Macmillan Co., 1897), p. 37, says: "Strong as was the town organization, it was not older than the central governments, and it cannot be said that the State was founded on the towns," he could not have had in mind the settlement of this State.

Arnold, p. 487, says:

"Before that period" (the combination under the first charter) "each town was in itself sovereign and enjoyed a full measure of civil and religious freedom."

The original colonies of Rhode Island have, therefore, enjoyed a period of independent sovereignty as separate towns, and two of them as a union of towns, although the united colony and the State never have.

"But in the scattered communities which grew up on Rhode Island soil between 1636 and 1647, there were lacking not only organic law in common, but even documentary agreement in common, and also any delegation of authority from outside their limits,—until the patent, whose provisions went into effect in 1647." (Foster's Town Government in Rhode Island, 12.)

As was well said in "The Nation," 39 vol. p. 117:

"The diversity of character and interest in the smallest of the colonies is another illustration of the truth taught by Greek and Italian history, that it is not always the largest States that afford the most instructive data for political history."

Milton, that profound political thinker as well as poet, in his pamphlet entitled "Ready and Easy Way to Establish a Free Commonwealth," said, in language pregnant with meaning:

"Nothing can be more essential to the freedom of a people than to have the administration of justice and all public ornaments in their own election and within their own bounds, without long traveling or depending upon remote places to obtain their right or any civil accomplishment, so it be not supreme but subordinate to the general power and union of the whole republic: in which happy firmness, as in the particular above mentioned, we shall also far exceed the United Provinces, by having, not as they do, to the retarding and distracting oftimes of their counsels on urgent occasions, many sovereignties united in one commonwealth, but many commonwealths under one united and entrusted sovereignty." (2 Milton Prose Works, Boston, 1826, 299.)

It is well known that Milton and Roger Williams were friends, and saw much of each other on Williams' visits to England. We have Williams' own testimony that he taught Milton Dutch, and in return Milton read him "many more languages." In imagination

6

we see these two great souls communing over the establishment of these colonies, holding forth " a lively experiment that a flourishing civil state may stand and be best maintained with full liberty in religious concernments," and it may be that it was Williams' report to Milton of the success of that experiment in Rhode Island that led him to write the above.

Bryce says, speaking of Rhode Island :

" This singular little commonwealth whose area is 1,085 square miles (less than that of Ayrshire or Antrim) is, of all the American States, that which has furnished the most abundant analogies to the Greek republics of antiquity, and which deserves to have its annals treated of by a philosophic historian."
(1 Am. Commw. 18.)

Bancroft, our great historian, vol. 1, p. 380, has well said :

" The annals of Rhode Island if written in the spirit of philosophy, would exhibit the forms of society under a peculiar aspect : had the territory of the State corresponded to the importance and singularity of the principles of its early existence, the world would have been filled with wonder at the phenomena of its history."

The existence of towns was an admitted underlying fact when the parlimentary charter of 1647 and the royal charter of 1663 were accepted, and there arose an unwritten constitution, a part of which was the right of the towns to administer their own local affairs. The extent and variety of these powers of self-control over their own local affairs far exceeded those of any other State, and they continue in force at the present day in Rhode Island in nearly their full vigor.

But it will be claimed that such a doctrine is incompatible with the doctrine of State sovereignty ; that it goes too far, because if accepted it would result in establishing a new sovereign, i. e. town sovereignty, in addition to State sovereignty and national sovereignty.

It is time the false and misleading notion of State sovereignty were laid at rest. In truth, a State of the United States is not a sovereign. There is but one sovereign in this country, and that is the United States (Jameson, 65), or, more properly, the people of the United States.

" There has never been a time in our history when the States were sovereign."
(Jameson, 51.)

Madison is reported to have said, in the federal convention in 1787 :

"The States never possessed the essential rights of sovereignty. These were always vested in congress. Their voting, as States, in congress, is no evidence of sovereignty. The State of Maryland voted by counties. Did this make the counties sovereign ? The States at present are only great corporations, having the power of making laws, and these are effectual only if they are not contradictory to the general confederation."

That no State ever was sovereign was affirmed by the supreme court of the United States in 1795. (Penhallow v. Doane's Admrs. 3 Dall. 54, 80.)

"If it be asked, in whom, during our revolutionary war, was lodged and by whom was exercised, this supreme authority ? No one will hesitate for an answer. It was lodged in and exercised by congress ; it was there or nowhere ; the States individually did not, and with safety could not, exercise it. * * * *"

So Jay, C. J. said in Chisholm Excr. v. State of Georgia, 2 Dall. 419 (471) :

" 'We the *people of the* United States, do ordain and establish this constitution.' " Here we see the people acting as sovereigns of the whole country, and in the language of sovereignty establishing a constitution by which it was their will that the State governments should be bound and to which the State constitutions should be made to conform. * * The truth is, that the States individually, were not known nor recognized as sovereign, by foreign nations, nor are they now ; the States collectively, under congress, as the connecting point, or head, were acknowledged by foreign powers, as sovereign." (See also Story, Com. on Const. § § 210–216.)

That no State is or ever was sovereign results also from the fact that no State is or ever was independent. It was a joint independence by the people of all the States they won, not a several independence of any one State, nor of the people of any one State. In the opinion last quoted Jay, C. J., said, also (do. 470) :

"From the crown of *Great Britain* the sovereignty of their country passed to the people of it. * * * In establishing it (the constitution) the people exercised their own rights and their own proper sovereignty ; and conscious of the plenitude of it, they declared with becoming dignity ! 'We *the people of the United States* do ordain and establish this constitution.' "

So Wilson, J., in Chisholm v. Georgia, 2 Dall. 419 at 454, said, speaking also of the people of the United States :

" They *might* have announced themselves 'SOVEREIGN' people of the *United States :* But serenely conscious of the *fact* they avoided the *ostentatious declaration.*

We must not allow ourselves to be misled by the conventional manner in which we speak of *State sovereignty.* All that we really mean in using the term is the exercise of the highest powers of the State within the limits allowed by the constitution and laws of the United States, and at most this can only be characterized as a limited sovereignty. There can then, therefore, be no objection to saying that within certain limits the town in Rhode Island is and always has been sovereign. We make no such affirmation of the towns in all the States of the Union. Mushroom growths of a day, some of the States undoubtedly have complete powers over their towns and cities that never existed until they created them. But no general rules of law can be founded, as to all towns, by cases arising in the courts in such States. They have no such historic past, no such a course of constitutional development running back to the beginning of our country and even before any State or colony of Rhode Island existed. It is not too much to say that had such a system of town government existed throughout the country as has been shown to have existed in this State, and had the people known such a system, the doctrine of States' rights would never have become established, and there probably would have been no secession of States and no civil war. Traces of the mischievous doctrine are still to be found, however, where one would least expect them. Art. IX Const. of R. I. gives, as the form of oath to be taken by all general officers :

"You * * * do solemnly swear (or affirm) to be true and faithful unto this State, and to support the constitution of this State and of the United States. * *"

Was it mere harmless vanity or some lingering disposition to rank the State before the United States that led to this order? Of course it is logically incorrect. The constitution of the United States being the supreme law of the land, should always come first, for in case of conflict between the two, the provisions of the constitution of the State must give way to those of the constitution of the United States.

Early in the summer of 1643, Roger Williams embarked for England from New York in a Dutch ship, being compelled to this course by the refusal of Massachusetts to permit him to pass through their limits or to take passage in one of their vessels. He had been selected by the Rhode Island government and that of Providence to procure a charter for both governments. He succeeded in his efforts and returned in 1644, bringing with him the charter uniting the three colonies of Providence, Portsmouth and Newport, as "The Incorporation of Providence Plantations in the Narragansett Bay, in New England."

It was not until May, 1647, that the freemen from the four towns or colonies, Providence, Portsmouth, Newport, and Warwick met in Portsmouth, accepted the charter and formed a government thereunder for the united colony that afterwards became the State. Fortunately the records are preserved. They should be studied and understood by every voter in Rhode Island. (1 R. I. Col. Recs. 147 to 207.)

This first meeting of the corporators to accept the charter was, in fact, what the name imports, a general assembly of the whole body of freemen. The record states: "It was voted and found that the major part of the colony were present at this assembly, whereby was full power to transact." It was agreed that a quorum of forty might "act as if the whole were present and be of as full authority." The general assembly being thus organized: "It was agreed that all should set their hands to an engagement to the charter." The representative system was then adopted by ordering that "a week before any general court, notice should be given to every town by the head officer that they choose a committee for the transaction of the affairs there," and they provided for a proxy vote in the words "and such as go not may send their votes sealed." They then adopted a remarkable code of laws, and elected general officers by ballot, to continue in office for one year or till new be chosen.

The growth of Warwick had been hindered by dissensions among its founders; an attempted surrender of jurisdiction, by some of the settlers, to Massachusetts; the foray from Massachusetts of officers and forty soldiers that captured the Gortonists after a siege, carried them as prisoners to Boston, where they were tried for heresy and sedition and found guilty, as "blasphemous enemies of the true religion of our Lord Jesus Christ and His holy ordinances, and also of all civil authority among the people of God, and particularly in this jurisdiction."

Gorton and six others were sentenced to be confined in irons during the pleasure of the court, to be set to work, and to suffer death should they break jail or in any way proclaim heresy or reproach to the church or State. Their cattle were appraised and sold to defray the cost of seizure and trial. Massachusetts continued her claim of jurisdiction over Warwick until 1665, warning against any one's settling there without leave of their general court, forbidding the return of the Gortonists after their release from jail and placing their houses at the disposal of petitioners for the Warwick land.

Extract from report of the king's commissioners concerning the New England colonies, made December, 1665:

"The Matachusetts did maintain Pumham (a petty sachim in this Province) twenty yeares against this Colony, and his chiefe sachim, and did by armed soldiers besiege and take prisoners Mr. Gorton, Howden. Wykes. Greene and others in this Province, and carry'd them to Boston, put them in chaines, and took eighty head of cattle from them, for all which they could never yet get satisfaction."
(John Carter Brown, MSS. 1. No. 63.)

But, in 1647, at the meeting to accept the charter granted to Roger Williams, Warwick was admitted to the union, although not named in the charter, the record being: "It was agreed that Warwick should have the same privileges as Providence" (2 R. I. Col. Recs. 148), thus furnishing a precedent for the admission of other towns afterwards, and putting them all on the same footing.

In 1648:

"Upon the petition and humble request of the freemen of the Towne of Providence, exhibited unto this present session of the General Assembly, wherein they desire freedome and libertie to incorporate themselves into a body politicke, and we, the said Assembly, having duly weighed and seriously considered the premises, and being willing and ready to provide for the ease and libertie of the people, have thought fit and by the authoritie aforesaid, and by these presents, do give grant and confirme unto the free inhabitants of the towne of Providence, a free and absolute charter of civill incorporation and government to be knowne by the Incorporation of Providence Plantation in the Narragansett Bay in New England, together with full power and authoritie to governe and rule themselves, and such others as shall hereafter inhabit within any part of the said Plantation, by such a form of civil government as by voluntarie consent of all, or the greater part of them, shall be found most suitable unto their estate and condition : and, to that end, to make and ordaine such civil orders and constitutions, to inflict such punishments upon transgressors, and for execution thereof, and of the common statute lawes of the colonye agreed unto and the penalties, and so many of them as are not annexed already unto the colonye courte of trialls, so to place and displace officers of justice, as they or the greater part of them shall, by one consent, agree unto. Provided, nevertheless, that the said lawes, constitutions and punishments, for the civil gov of the said plantation, be conformable to the lawes of England, so f ure and

General assembly... of the... shall... pleasure...

Speakes in his annals of Providence...

...In 1633 the general assembly... passed an act the title of which was significant.

"An act... Council of the Town of Providence."

This title shows clearly that the general assembly did not attempt to *confer powers* upon the town, but simply to *recognize* and *explain* those it already possessed.

In 1832, upon the request of the citizens and representatives of Providence, a charter, drafted by a committee of its own citizens, was granted by the general assembly. Section I provided that "the inhabitants of the town of Providence shall continue to be a body politic and corporate by the name of 'The City of Providence.'"

It will be seen from this that Providence, until very lately the only city in the State, was not *created* nor *incorporated* by the general assembly. It simply *continued* it as a body politic and corporate under another name. "The Town of Providence" became "The City of Providence." It parted with no old rights to the general assembly, it acquired no new ones from it. The general assembly, at the request of the town of Providence moulded and directed its name and form so that it became the city of Providence.

The controversy between Rhode Island and Massachusetts over the next town admitted to Rhode Island (Westerly, in 1669) is illustrative of the fact already shown—that the early towns of Rhode Island were first settled and afterwards admitted to the union. Massachusetts claimed the whole Pequot country by right of conquest, and erected the tract on both sides of Pawcatuck river, which is now the westerly boundary of Rhode Island, into the township of Southertown, and attached it to the county of Suffolk. In 1660, William Vaughn and others, of Newport, bought part of this land, called Misquamicock, afterwards Westerly, of the Indians, and thirty-six settlers from Rhode Island took possession. Upon complaint to the Massachusetts general court from settlers on the east side of Pawcatuck river, a warrant was issued to the constable of Southertown to arrest the trespassers. They were taken to Boston and committed for want of bail. They were tried, sentenced to pay a fine of forty pounds, to be imprisoned until it was paid, and to give sureties for one hundred pounds to keep the peace. Rhode Island denied the right of Massachusetts to the jurisdiction asserted, and a controversy arose between the two colonies. Connecticut joined, ordering the inhabitants of Mystic and Pawcatuck not to exercise authority under commissions from any other colony. In 1663 a house was torn down by residents of Southertown because it was claimed to be within the asserted jurisdiction of Rhode Island. William Marble, a deputy from the marshal of Suffolk, bearing a letter to the Westerly settlers on this subject, was arrested, sent to Newport, and confined in prison eleven months. In 1665 a royal commission, appointed to settle these and other controversies, decided that no lands conquered from the natives should be disposed of by any colony unless the conquest was just and the soil was included in the charter of the colony, and that no colony should attempt to exercise jurisdiction beyond its chartered limits. This put an end to the asserted right of jurisdiction of Massachusetts. (1 Arnold, Hist. R. I. 276, 282, 316.)

May, 1669, the general assembly voted:

"This Court taking notice of the returne by the committee, to wit: Mr. John Easton, Mr. Benjamin Smith, James Greene, Edward Smith, Caleb Carr and William Weeden, in reference to the petition or desire of the people inhabiting at Musquamacott and Pawcatuck in the King's Province, to be made a towneshipp, it being and lying within this jurisdiction, as by his Majestyes Letters Pattents it may appear, and considering the Power by his Majesty given to this Assembly to order and settle townes, cityes and corporations, within this said Jurisdiction, as shall seem meet * * * Be it therefore enacted by this Assembly, and by the authority thereof that * * * shall be knowne and called by the name of Westerly; and shall be reputed and deemed the fifth town of this Collony: and shall have, vse and enjoy all such privilidges, and exercise all such methods and formes for the well ordering their towne affaires as any other towne in this Collony may now vse and exercise : and they shall have liberty to elect and send two Deputyes to sitt and act in the Genneral Assemblyṣ of this Collony from time to time * * * ." (2 R. I. Col. Recs. 250–251.)

The settlement of Block Island, its history and incorporation as New Shoreham, the sixth town, still further illustrates this.

At first under the jurisdiction of Massachusetts, it was granted to Gov. Endicott and three others, in 1658, as a reward for their public services. They sold it in 1661 to Simon Ray and eight associates, who began a settlement there in 1662, liquidated the Indian title subject to a reservation in favor of the natives, and set apart one-sixteenth of the land for the support of a minister forever. One Dr. Alcock also claimed title to the island, by purchasé of "some in Boston (who took upon them power never granted them to sell it)." (2 R. I. Col. Recs., 128.) Under the charter of 1663 Block Island became a part of Rhode Island. In 1664 it was

"Resolved by this Assembly : That the Governor and Deputy Governor be desired to send to Block Island to declare vnto our frends the inhabitants thereof, that they are vnder our care, and that they admitt not of any other to beare rule over them but the power of this Collony." (2 R. I. Col. Recs. 32.)

Petitions were presented to the general assembly in 1664 by the inhabitants of the island, for admission as freemen of the colony. They were referred to a committee which reported a letter that was sent, and may be found in 2 R. I. Col. Recs. 53, setting forth in detail how the inhabitants are to be admitted and sworn in as freemen of the colony. November 6, 1672, the island was incorporated as New Shoreham, "as signs of our unity and likeness to many parts of our native country." The act (2 R. I. Col. Recs. 55, 466–470) expressly recognizes their existing form of government and continues some of its features. This is still the law.

Although under the jurisdiction of Rhode Island since 1663, Block Island continued to govern itself in all matters until 1672, and the act incorporating it well deserves study from the light it throws upon the way in which this little isolated community had worked out its own system of government, retained part of it when it was incorporated, and has continued to exercise it ever since, even gaining admission of its established right to exemption from military duty ("until otherwise prescribed by law") in Art. XIV, Sec. 4, of the constitution of 1842, still in force.

By the act of incorporation the inhabitants were required

"To meete four times in the yeare for their said towne affaires, for the making of such order or bye lawes as may be needfull for their better management of their affaires among themselves according to their constitution, not opuginge the laws of his Majestie's realme of England, his patent, nor the laws of this colony, agreeable thereto."

On account of the distance by sea, so that often the inhabitants could not reach the mainland "because of danger and hinderings divers ways," the wardens were empowered, following their custom already established before their incorporation, "to hold pleas of actions of account, debt, detinue, trespass and of the case to the value of five pounds sterling of New England money," * * "and to proceed in the said actions according to the lawes of his Majestie's realme of England (so farr as the constitution of the place will admitt) and accordinge to due forme of lawe in this Collony agreeable thereto."

"The remoteness of the island rendered it almost independent of the colony, and produced a different system from that which prevailed in the other towns." (1 Arnold, Hist. R. I. 304.)

The wardens of New Shoreham still join persons in marriage in the town, a privilege not enjoyed in any other town in the State.

It is evident this town was not the creature of the State, but came into it with established powers of its own that it still continues to enjoy. (Gen. Laws R. I. cap. 191, sec. 8.)

King's Towne, afterwards Kingston, now North and South Kingstown, the seventh town, was settled in 1641. In October, 1674, it was

"Voted by the King's authority in this Assembly, it is approved the General Councill's acts in obstructinge Connecticutt Colony from useinge jurisdiction in the Narragansett country and the Councill's establishing a towneshipp there, and the calling it Kingstown, with liberty as hath been granted to New Shoreham; * * * * and that futurely it shall be lawfull to summons as many of our inhabitants as they see cause to attend at Narragansett to oppose Connecticut from useinge jurisdiction there: but not in any hostile manner, or to kill or hurt any person." (2 R. I. Col. Recs. 525.)

In 1679 it was

"Voted, the Recorder shall draw forth the copy of the act of the Generall Assembly in October, 1674, concerninge the confirming of the act of the Generall Council, in establishing a towneshipp in Narragansett, and calling it King's Towne, which shall be sent to the inhabitants there, under the seale of the Collony." (3 R. I. Col. Recs. 55.)

East Greenwich, the eighth town, was incorporated in 1677. This would seem to be the first town that was incorporated first and settled afterwards.

Arnold, p. 428, says:

" A tract of five thousand acres was laid out in two parts, one of five hundred acres on the bay, for house lots, and the remainder in farms of ninety acres each, and distributed among fifty men, who were now incorporated as the town of East Greenwich."
(See the act, 2 R. I. Col. Recs. 586.)

At 588 it declares:

" And to the end that the said persons and their successors, the proprietors of the said land from time to time, may be in the better capacity to manage their public affairs, this Assembly doe enact and declare that the said plantation shall be a towne, by the name and title of East Greenwich, in his Majesty's Collony of Rhode Island and Providence Plantations, with all rights, libertys and priviledges whatsoever unto a towne appertaininge."

Jamestown, the island the Indian name of which was Quononoquitt (now Conanicut), was incorporated as the ninth town, in 1678, although it was settled before then. The record is very brief:

" Voted, That the petition of Mr. Caleb Carr and Mr. Francis Brinley, on the behalfe of themselves and the proprietors for Quononoqutt Island to be made a towneship, shall be first adjetated and debated.

Voted, That the said petition is granted; and that the said Quononoqutt shall be a towneship, with the like priviledges and libertyes granted to New Shoreham."

Some of the peculiar features of its town government are still preserved, protected by law. It still elects its wardens, whose " warden's courts " have the same jurisdiction as the district courts in other parts of the State. (Gen. L. R. I. cap. 228, § 24.)

No further change as to towns took place until 1730, when " an act for erecting and incorporating the outlands of the town of Providence into three towns " was passed. (4 R. I. Col. Recs. 442.) Smithfield, Scituate, and Glocester were thus incorporated; and, in language almost identical with that cited above in the acts incorporating the previous towns, it was enacted " and that the inhabitants thereof from time to time (in the case of Glocester ' for the time being ') shall have and enjoy the like benefits and privileges (or liberty) with other towns in this colony, according to our charter (or agreeably to our charter—or by our charter do)."

These citations are enough to sustain our contention that as new towns were incorporated they were granted the same benefits, privileges, and liberties that were enjoyed by the four original towns or colonies that existed before there was any united colony, and that they came into that united colony with certain well-established rights, one of which was the right to manage their own local affairs.

The following letter, written in 1832 by John Howland, is significant. A soldier in the revolutionary war, he settled in Providence after it was over, followed the humble profession of a barber, and lived to great old age. A self-educated man, he left his mark on the city, being the founder of the Providence Institution for Savings, the principal savings bank in Rhode Island, and its first president. In this letter to Rev. James Knowles, he said:

"You ask me for a copy of the act incorporating the town. I have not yet searched for it, but intend to. If I had lived in those days, I should have opposed receiving such an act from the general assembly. The four original towns made the general assembly, and they could confer no power which was not already possessed by the old towns. New towns might be incorporated, but it was absurd for the old ones to receive authority from their own agents or deputies. We saw and felt the disadvantages of this pretended act of incorporation two or three years ago when the school bill was discussed and passed. The assembly then claimed the power to restrict the towns from levying taxes for the support of schools, as they said no such power was granted them in their acts of incorporation and that all the power of the towns was derived from special acts of the general assembly. 'But the truth is the old towns had, from their first settlement the power to assess taxes for this as well as for other purposes, and they did not relinquish it when they received their corporate powers. The acts of incorporation could not grant or restrict, but only confirm the powers already existing, which were not contrary to the laws of England."

(Stone, Life and Rec. John Howland, 256.)

This man understood thoroughly, not from books, but from his practical knowledge derived from a long life under the institutions he wrote about, the Rhode Island ideas about local self-government. He represented what has always been the common understanding of the people of the State, and the entire past legislation of the State has voiced that understanding.

We are in a better position now to call more particular attention to the analogy between the system of towns forming Rhode Island and the system of States forming the United States. This analogy is most remarkable. As the original thirteen States constituted the Union of the United States, so did the four original colonies or towns constitute the united colony, subsequently the State. As new States came into the Union, so new towns became a part of Rhode Island. Out of the union of the towns arose the the colony, subsequently the State, that afterwards admitted or created new towns. Out of the union of the States arose the United States, that, in its turn, created or admitted new States into the Union. Each town of this State and each State of the United States is supreme in its own sphere, each regulating and administering its own internal affairs, thus constituting a hierarchy consisting of: 1, the town; 2, the State; 3, the United States. When a new State came into the Union, it reserved its local self-government, as the thirteen original States had reserved it before them. So, when new towns were formed in Rhode Island, they became a part of the State upon same footing with the four original towns, that is to say, they retained the right to local self-government by implication, since no distinction was made between the power of the original towns and of the new towns. So no distinction is made, once inside the Union, between an original State and a new State.

"The similarity between the New England confederacy of 1643 and the National Confederation of 1783 has been often remarked ; but there is yet a stronger resemblance in the relative position of the four towns of Rhode Island in 1647 and the States of the Federal Union under the constitution of 1787."
(1 Arnold 211 note.)

The admission of new towns to the union, with like powers as if they were original towns, still further marks this analogy:

"This colony has, in fact, been a sort of microcosm, in which there have been developed, on a smaller scale, the more important issues which have operated in a large way on the stage of national government."
(Foster, Town Government in Rhode Island, 35.)

In an address by George Bancroft, the historian, before the New York Historical Society, in 1866, he said: "more ideas which have since become national have emanated from the little colony of Rhode Island than from any other."

This power of the towns of this State to local self-government can no more be taken from the new towns than from the old towns ; for all, once inside the united colony, or State, are on the same footing, just as all the States in the Union, new and old, are on the same footing. The existence of towns with powers of self-government was an admitted underlying fact when the parliamentary charter of 1643 and the royal charter of 1663 were granted, and there has arisen an unwritten constitution, through the continuous and uninterrupted usage of two hundred and sixty years, a part of which is the right of the towns in Rhode Island to administer their own local affairs. The extent and variety of these powers of self-control by the towns of this State far exceeded those of the towns of any other State, and, unrecognized by jurists, they continue in force at the present day, in something like their pristine vigor. Two reasons have contributed largely to long continued ignorance of these powers, not only in Rhode Island, but similarly in other States throughout New England, New York, Pennsylvania, and other of the original States. In the first place, the success of the revolution exalted the power of the States, forgetful of the fact that the towns contributed as much as the States to our success. But for Samuel Adams and the organized exertion by him and others of the powers of the towns throughout New England, the revolution would have lost one of its most powerful supports. In the next place, the absence of printed records of the doings of the founders of our towns and colonies until a late day, has prevented the growth of a body of lawyers trained in the constitutional law of their respective States. Only a few mousing antiquaries have known anything about these matters until within the last generation. Consequently there has not been any educated public opinion, even among those competent to pass upon such subjects, until lately, that could keep alive a knowledge of these principles and prevent encroachment upon them. Law after law by legislature after legislature in State after State has little by little restricted the town power in a way that cannot be defended. The decisions in such a State as Massachusetts show an ignorance of these principles of their local constitutional law only to be accounted for upon the supposition that they did not know the history of their own State.

(See, e. g., the case of Commonwealth v. Plaisted 148 Mass. 375.)

In that State the rights of the towns to local self-government not having been protected by the judiciary, we find more than 750 special laws passed by the general court to regulate the local affairs of the city of Boston alone.

In consequence of the decisions of her courts, especially that in Commonwealth v. Plaisted, 148 Mass. 375 (1889), the glory of Massachusetts as a union of self-governing towns is gone, never to return, except through a constitutional amendment or a reversal of that case upon re-argument and submission of authorities. For an examination of the briefs in the social law library in Boston confirms the suspicion, which the opinion aroused, that the argument herein presented was not presented to the court, nor were any authorities sustaining these views before the court.

The opinion cannot be considered, therefore, as being one of weight or in any way worthy of the reputation of this able court.

Formerly the bar and bench did not know the political history and the constitutional development of the different States, because the records from which alone such knowledge could be acquired were not in print. Herein lies the advantage of printing in the most complete and ample form all the records of the founders of all our towns as well as States, a duty that has not even yet been duly performed as it should be. But the printing of our colonial records, even in their present imperfect shape, has made it possible for the lawyers of the present day to know much more about the development of the constitutional law in Rhode Island than the generation before us could possibly know. It behooves us, therefore, to help to form a better enlightened public opinion on these matters. The object of this pamphlet will be achieved if anything herein contributes to that end and will help to bring about a better government for this State.

Although the general assembly has undoubted power to pass general laws affecting all towns and cities alike, or, upon the request of any one town or city, to give it additional power; although it may mould and direct by general laws all towns and cities, or even any one of them, upon request or necessity—it is submitted that in Rhode Island towns are the recognized units of its political system; cities are but towns in which the increased population has rendered impracticable the control and regulation of local affairs by town-meetings and town councils, and the inhabitants have therefore petitioned the general assembly to place such control in a city council; a city in Rhode Island is but a town that has asked for and submitted to a city organization: it is a political unit in which the control theretofore exercised by town-meetings has now, at their own request, become vested in a city council, with a mayor as the executive head.

If it has become desirable to change a town into a city, to change town boundaries or to divide a town to make two towns, the power thus to mould and direct has been exercised by the general assembly, but only upon the request of the parties in interest, and subject to their assent. Such as decision as that in Philadelphia *v.* Fox, 64 Penn. St. 169 (1870), would be impossible in Rhode Island. It was there held that the city of Philadelphia is merely an agency instituted by the sovereign for the purpose of carrying out in detail the objects of government, subject to the control of the legislature, who may even destroy its very existence with the mere breath of arbitrary discretion. "*Sic voleo, sic jubeo*, that is all the sovereign authority need say," says so eminent a judge as Sharswood, at p. 180.

It is no wonder that in States where such decisions as these are made, all sense of civic pride is gone, all power of self-control being taken away, and consequently the government has passed into the hands of professional politicians, many of whom, if they received their deserts, should be behind the bars of the State prison.

A like fate awaits us in Rhode Island if we tamely submit to the continued encroachments of the general assembly, under the leadership of the dominant political party and the machine behind it.

But, it is urged, Boston is a democratic city, and this decision was necessary to keep that city under the control of the republican general court! The same argument was heard in the State house in Providence last spring. It was urged that the bill to authorize the governor to appoint a board of police and license commissioners for the city of Providence must be carried through, because Providence is a democratic city, and this measure would keep it under the control of the republican general assembly! Considerations of this nature may appeal to machine politicians, but they certainly will not to any honest believer in our form of government who places the welfare of the State above party and party success.

In England the civil divisions into counties, hundreds tithings and towns date as far back as Alfred the Great. They were substantially in existence before the Norman conquest. The Anglo-Saxon race carried with it everywhere their Teutonic institutions, their system of local self-government. "It is here they have acquired the habits of subordination and obedience to the laws, of patient endurance, resolute purpose, and the knowledge of civil government which distinguish them from every other government." (State *v.* Denny, 118 Ind. 118 at 458.) The townsfolk themselves assessed their taxes, levied them in their own way and paid them through their own officers. They claimed broad rights of justice, whether by ancient custom or royal grant; criminals were brought before the mayor's court, and the town prison, with irons and its cage, testified to an authority which ended only with death. (Green, Town Life in the Fifteenth Century, 2.)

But in England, as well as in the United States, there was a falling off from their former high estate. There, as here, there was no printed record of their ancient procedure and authority, no trained body of lawyers versed in the constitutional law of town rights. "Four hundred years later the very remembrance of their free and vigorous life was utterly blotted out. When commissioners were sent in 1835 to enquire into the position of the English boroughs, there was not one community where the ancient traditions still lived." (do. p. 5.)

The supremacy of the town in Rhode Island is also evidenced by the insignificant role the county has always filled in this State.

The first division into counties was in 1703.

"Be it further enacted by the authority aforesaid : That there shall be two inferior Courts of Common Pleas to be holden on the main land for her majesty, early in the county known by the name of Providence Plantations ; and that it shall be held at Providence first as the shire town ; and next at the town of Warwick."

(3 R. I. Col. Recs. 477–1703.)

"Be it further enacted by the authority aforesaid : That Rhode Island, with the rest of the islands within the said Collony, shall be a county by the name of Rhode Island County ; and that Newport be the shire town."

(3 R. I. Col. Recs. 478–1703.)

It will be noticed that here there was no incorporation of the counties—they were merely geographical divisions of the colony. Washington county, originally called the Narragansett country, was created next, in 1729, as King's county (4 R. I. Col. Recs. 427). The act is entitled "An act for the dividing the colony of Rhode Island and Providence Plantations into three counties * * * *" (Newport, Providence, and King's county), and was passed because "the more remote inhabitants are put to great trouble and difficulty in prosecuting their affairs in the common course of justice, as the courts are now established," and this is the only end achieved even now by the division of the State into counties. The name of this county was changed to Washington county in 1781.

The next county created was Bristol county, in 1747 (5 R. I. Col. Recs. 208), and the fifth and last county was Kent county, in 1750 (5 R. I. Col. Recs, 302).

But although we speak of these counties as incorporated (it is noteworthy that not all of these acts do so), they are not corporations in the sense that towns are corporations—for in Rhode Island everything is done by the towns and nothing by the counties.

We have no county commissioners, no county records, no county taxes, no county roads, no county probate courts. All these things are and ever have been managed by the towns. The only county officers are the clerk of the supreme court and court of common pleas, who has the custody of the papers of these courts when they meet in the different counties; the sheriff of the county, whose writ, however, runs throughout the State; and the keeper of the county jail, who, in other than Providence county, is the sheriff of the county. A county can neither sue nor be sued in Rhode Island, as a town can, and is not a corporation.

The power of the town over its own probate matters is another mark of the supremacy of the town in Rhode Island and of the continued retention of an original power. Until the acceptance of the charter, in 1647, each town had jurisdiction over probate matters arising in the town, as it had over all other judicial matters.

In "that remarkable piece of colonial legislation, the code of 1647" (Gleanings from the Judicial History of Rhode Island, by Judge Durfee, 6), passed at the first meeting of the general assembly, we find (1 R. I. Col. Recs. 188) a statute concerning the probate of wills, conferring this power upon "the head officer of the Towne" whom we should now call the president of the town council, and who was the chief executive of each town.

In 1675 it was

"Voted, whereas by law of this collony (in the letters thereof in the said law) bearing date in the yeare 1647, said saith, the probate of wills, was to be before the head officer, which said name (in the said law) by the present constitutions is extinct, and by reason of difference of opinion probation of wills is deferred; and for that the thinge is as weighty as to make a will for the dead, dyinge without a will, and the said supposed head officer may be in his own case; therefore be it enacted, that the power of probation of wills shall be in the Towne Councills or major part of each, to which it doth belong."

(2 R. I. Col. Recs. 525.)

This law plainly recognizes and restores a former custom, and as thus established it has continued to be the law even until now, special probate courts being instituted by the general assembly only as increase of population requires.

The life of the towns of Rhode Island has been continuous and uninterrupted since their respective settlements, that of Providence being in 1636; of Portsmouth, 1637; of Newport, 1638; and of Warwick, 1642–3. This cannot be said of the colony and State. In 1651 William Coddington, an uneasy and ambitious spirit, the first judge in Portsmouth, 1638 to 1639, the first judge in Newport, 1639 to 1640, and the first governor under the union of these two colonies, from 1640 to 1647, went to England, and by means now impossible to discover, obtained from the council of State a commission to govern the islands of Rhode Island and Conanicut during his life, with a council of six men to be named by the people and approved by himself. It made him the autocrat of the fairest and wealthiest portion of the colony, and put an end to the united colony for the time being. The alarm was great, and John Clarke was appointed the agent of the island towns, Portsmouth and Newport, to procure a repeal of Coddington's commission, and Roger Williams was appointed the agent of the main land towns, Providence and Warwick, to obtain a confirmation of the charter of 1643.

" In effect the same result was aimed at and secured—a return to their former mode of government by a reunion under the charter."
(Arnold, 239.)

They succeeded in their mission, and upon receipt of intelligence of the repeal of Coddington's power a town-meeting was held in Providence February 20, 1652–3, at which, in accordance with a request from the town of Warwick, a meeting of commissioners of the two towns was agreed upon. It was held at Pawtuxet the following week. They drafted a reply to a letter from the island towns of Portsmouth and Newport relating to a reunion of the colony, and appointed two members from each town to carry it and to consult with those of the island concerning the peace and welfare of the State (1 R. I. Col. Rec. 239). But their labor was fruitless. The main land towns contended they were the Providence Plantations, their charter never having been vacated and their government having continued uninterrupted by the defection of the island towns, and therefore the general assembly should meet with them. The island towns claimed the assembly should meet there because they formed the greater part of the colony and hence had a larger interest in the matter.

The result was that two distinct general assemblies convened at the same time in 1653 and elected different general officers for the colony. So great was the feeling that the assembly at Providence disfranchised those who owned the validity of commissions to fight against the Dutch, issued by the other assembly. The dissension continued, and Sir Henry Vane wrote to the people of Rhode Island a most kind and imploring letter, urging them to reconcile their feuds, for the honor of God and the good of their fellow men. "Are there no wise men among you? No public self-denying spirits," he asks, * * * "who can find some way or means of union * * * before you become a prey to enemies?" The interest that Vane took in this matter was due to his intimacy with Williams, and because mainly through his friendly intervention the parliamentary charter was obtained. (Diman, Oration and Essays, 133).

At length a reunion was effected in 1654 by articles of agreement signed by a court or general assembly of six commissioners from each of the four towns, assembled at Warwick.

The administration or usurpation of Andros lasted two years and four months, from December 1686, to April 1689, during which time all the charter governments of New England were suspended.

Arnold, 1st vol. 487, says:

"The American system of town governments which necessity had compelled Rhode Island to initiate, fifty years before, now became the means of preserving the liberty of the individual citizen when that of the state or colony was crushed. To provide for this was the last act of the expiring legislature. For this purpose it was declared 'lawful for the freemen of each town in this colony to meet together and appoint five, or more or fewer, days in the year for their assembling together, as the freemen of each town shall conclude to be convenient, for the managing the affairs of their respective towns' and that yearly, upon one of those days, town officers should be chosen as heretofore, taxes levied, and other business transacted at such meetings, as the majority should determine."
(3 R. I. Col. Recs. 191.)

It was the towns, with their continuous existence, that kept alive the vital flame and rescued it from the embers of the dying colony, after three years of suspension of colonial corporate existence.

Discussion upon the referendum and the initiative is in vogue, but not even Oberholzer in his work on the subject calls attention to the fact that it was in Rhode Island in 1647, when the four already existing colonies organized under the parliamentary charter of 1644, the referendum was first introduced. The matter is of such importance as to require, for full understanding, the citation of the legislation adopted.

Among the "Acts and Orders Made and agreed upon at the Generall Court of Election held at Portsmouth in Rhode Island the 19, 20, 21 of May, Anno. 1647, for the Colonie and Province of Providence" (1 R. I. Col. Recs. 147), when the first charter was accepted, we find the following:

"2. It was Voted and found, that the major parte of the Colonie was present at this Assemblie, whereby there was full power to transact."

That is to say, this, the first meeting of the incorporated held formally to adopt the charter granted was, in fact, what the name imports, a general assembly of the whole people, and it then adopted the representative system. (It is to be remembered that the freemen from the towns continued thus to meet in Newport, either in person or by proxy, every May and October, and decided who should represent them in the general assembly for the next six months, until 1760.) (6 R. I. Col. Recs. 256.)

"7. It was unanimously agreed, That we do all owne and submit to the Lawes, as they are contracted in the Bulke with the Administration of Justice according thereto, which are to stand in force till the next Generall Courte of Election, and every Towne to have a Coppie of them, and then to present what shall appeare therein not to be suitable to the Constitution of the place, and then to amend it."

That is, whatever law of the general assembly was found not to conform to the constitution or compact of agreement of each town was to be amended. The freemen of the towns were jealous of their town rights, and took this means to preserve them.

"11. It is ordered, that all cases presented, concerning Generall Matters for the Colony, shall be first stated in the Townes, Vigd't, That is when a case is propounded: The Towne where it is propounded shall agitate and fully discuss the matter in their Towne Meetings and conclude by Vote: and then shall the Recorder of the Towne, or Towne Clerke, send a coppy of the agreement to every of the other three Townes, who shall agitate the case likewise in each Towne and vote it and collect the votes Then shall they commend it to the Committee for the General Courte (then a meeting called), who being assembled and finding the Major parte of the Colonie concurring in the case, it shall stand for a Law till the next Generall Assembly of all the people, then and there to be considered whether any longer to stand, yea or no: Further it is agreed, that six men of each Towne shall be the number of the Committee premised, and to be freely chosen. And further it is agreed, that when the General Courte thus assembled shall determine the cases before hand thus presented, It shall also be lawful for the said General Court, and hereby are they authorized, that if vnto them or any of them some case or cases shall be presented that may be deemed necessary for the public weale and good of the whole, they shall fully debate, discuss and determine ye matter among themselves: and then shall each Committee returning to their Towne declare what they have done in the case or cases premised. The Townes then debating and concluding, the votes shall be collected and sealed up, and then by the Towne Clarke of each Towne shall be sent with speed to the General Recorder, who, in the presence of the President shall open the votes: and if the major vote determine the case, it shall stand as a Law till the next General Assemblie then or there to be confirmed or nullified."

(1 R. I. Col. Recs. 148.)

It is believed that in this statute is found the earliest known instance of the initiative and referendum, now so much admired in the Swiss constitution.

Arnold (1 Hist. R. I. 203) says :

"The mode of passing general laws was then prescribed and deserves attention for the care with which it provides for obtaining a free expression of the opinions of the whole people. All laws were to be first discussed in the towns. The town first proposing it was to agitate the question in town meeting and conclude by vote. The town clerk was to send a copy of what was agreed on to the other three towns, who were likewise to discuss it and take a vote in town meeting. They then handed it over to a committee of six men from each town, freely chosen, which committee constituted the General Court, who were to assemble at a call for the purpose, and if they found a majority of the colony concurred in the case, it was to stand as a law, ' till the next General Assembly of all the people ' who were finally to decide whether it should continue as law or not. Thus the laws emanated directly from the people. The General Court had no power of revision over cases already presented, but simply the duty of promulgating the laws with which the towns had entrusted them. The right to originate legislation was, however, vested in them, to be carried out in this way. When the court had disposed of the matters for which it was called, should any case be presented upon which the public good seemed to require their action, they were to debate and decide upon it. Then each committee, on returning to their town, was to report the decision, which was to be debated and voted upon in each town ; the votes to be sealed and sent by each town clerk to the General Recorder, who, in presence of the President, was to count the votes. If a majority were found to have adopted the law, it was to stand as such till the next General Assembly should confirm or repeal it. The jealousy with which the people maintained their rights, and the checks thus put upon themselves in the exercise of the law-making power, as displayed in this preliminary act, present most forcibly the union of the two elements of liberty and law in the Rhode Island mind."

The law stood thus until 1650, when the following act was passed :

"Whereas, by the powre of the last General Assemblie for election, held at Newport in May last, where, by authority, an act was then established, that the

Representative Committee should have the full powre of ye Generall Assembly ; and who, when being lawfully mett, and orderly managed, did toward the latter end of that sessions, enact and give order for a new election of another representative, to assemble and sit with the like authoritie in October following : the which being accordingly now assembled and orderly managed, do by the authority and powre of the said ordinance, in the name and powre of the free people of this State, enact these lawes following.

It is ordered that from henceforth the representative committee being assembled and having enacted law or lawes, the said lawes shall be returned within six dayes after the breaking up or adjournment of that Assemblie ; and then within three days after the chiefe officer of the Towne shall call the Towne to the hearing of the Lawes so made ; and if any freeman shall mislike any law then made, they shall send their votes with their names fixed thereto vnto the General Recorder within tenn dayes after the reading of thoss lawes and no longer. And if itt appeare that the major vote within that time prefixed, shall come in and declare itt to be a nullity, then shall the Recorder signifie it to ye President, and the President shall forthwith signifie to ye Townes that such or such lawes is a null, and the silence to the rest shall be taken for approbation and confirmation of the lawes made : and it is ordered further, that the eleventh lawe made at Portsmouth, May 20, 21—1647 is repealed."

(1 R. I. Col. Recs. 228.)

In 1658 the law was changed, as follows :

" 12.   Whereas, it is conceived a wholesome liberty for the whole or major parte of the free inhabitants of this collony orderly to consider of the lawes made by the Commissioners' Courts : and upon finding discommodity in any law made by the sayd court, then orderly to show their dislike, and soe to invalid such a law.

It is therefore ordered and declared by this present Assembly, that from henceforth the Generall Recorder upon [such] pennalty as shall be Judged meete by a court of commissioners, shall send in to each towne a coppie of the lawes that are made at such courts, soe as they may be delivered to the Town Clarke of each towne within ten daies after the dissolution of each court from time to time ; and then the townes to have tenn daies time longer to meete and publish the sayd lawes, and to consider of them.   And in case the free inhabitants of each towne, or the major parte of them doe in a lawfull assembly vote down any law, and seale up the voates, and send them to the Generall Recorder within the sayd tenn daies : and that by the voates it doth appeare that the major parte of the people in each towne have so dissalowed it, then such a law to bee in noe force ; and otherwise if that bee not soe done within the twenty daies after the dissolution of each court, then all and every law to be in force : And however all to be in force that are not soe disannulled, and the townes shall pay the charge of sendinge the foresayd coppies.   Further, the Recorder is to open the sayd voates before the President, or in his absence, before the Assistant of the Towne where the Recorder lives, and then the President or such Assistant to give notice to the rest of the majestrates."

(1 R. I. Col. Recs. 401.)

This allowed ten days for the recorder to furnish each town clerk with a copy of the acts of the session, and ten more for the towns to consider them and, if they disapproved them, to notify the president and thus to annul the statute. The provision that any law not so disannulled was nevertheless to go into effect marked, however, the beginning of the decline of this peculiar system. Had it been provided that no law of the general assembly was to go into effect until approved by the towns, the system would have been more permanent.

In 1660 this was amended, as follows:

" Whereas, there is a certayne clause in a law made at Warwick, November the 2d 1658, toutching the people's libertie to disannull any law to them presented from the Courts of Commissioners, as there is premised : by which clause it seems the privilidges are not soe clearly evinced as the Commissioners thereby and therein did intend in formeinge the same law, in regard of this clawse (that the major parte of each Towne in the Collony must send in their voates of their towne to the Generall Recorder, to disallow any law that should be soe presented, within tenn daies after it is presented to the Towne, if they conceive such, or any such law not .wholesome). It is therefore ordered, by the authority of this present Assembly, that the aforesaid clause be rectified, and that instead thereof it be enacted, and it is hereby enacted, that there be three months time, that is to say, fowre score and six daies alowed for the returne of the voates from each towne unto the General Recorder after that such lawes be presented (in such order and time as by the foresayd law is provided) to each towne :

As alsoe wee further enact that it apearinge by the returne of the voates, that the major parte of the free inhabitants of this Collony have disapproved or disannulled any such law or lawes, then the sayd law or lawes to be of noe force ; although any one towne or other should be wholly silent therein, or otherwise such law or lawes to be in force according to the true intent of the other parte or clause in the abovesayd law of November the 2d 1658; and this foresayd addition to stand and be in full force, any law or lawes, or any clawes or clawses in any former law contayned, to the contrary notwithstandinge."

(1 R. I. Col. Recs. 429.)   •

Besides allowing more time to disannul a law (three months instead of ten days), a majority of all the votes in the colony was substituted in the place of a majority in each town. This was a great step towards consolidation of the united government.

The new charter was obtained in 1663, but it made no change in the relation of the towns to the colony. In 1664 :

"It is ordered and inacted by this Assembly. That whereas ther are severall lawes extant amongst our former lawes inconsistant with the present Government, as houlding of Courts of Commistions, and repealing of the acts of the General Assemblyes by votings in town meetings : together with severall other of licke natuer, which are contradictory to the forme of the present government, erected by his Majestyes gratious letters pattent, that all such lawes be declared null and voyd, and that all other lawes be of force vntil some other course be taken by a Generall Assembly for better provition hearein : and further, wee declare, that all obligations formerly taken to the Court of Trialles to be houlden in Newport, the second Tusday of this instant, March, be of full force and vertue to make each parson responsible to the sayd court."

(1 R. I. Col. Recs. 27.)

It is to be noticed that although this act annulled the laws under which the towns could annul the acts of the General Assembly, it was silent as to those laws under which the towns could initiate new laws. They would seem to have become extinct merely through non-use. It would seem, also, that the act was intended to be provisional only (" vntill some other course be taken by a General Assembly for better provition herein." " From these provisions," says Governor Hopkins, " came the common story, that some towns had heretofore repealed acts of the General Assembly." (7 R. I. Hist. Colls. 45.) This remark shows that at the time Gov-Hopkins wrote the people had forgotten what the original powers of the towns were. We find, therefore, that the power of the freemen of the towns to annul the laws passed by the general assembly lasted through the life of the first charter and was not abolished until after the adoption of the second charter, while the power of the freemen of the towns to initiate legislation has never been formally abolished, but is only lost through non-use. It is evident that the original towns or colonies of Rhode Island possessed governmental powers of their own before there was any united colony; that they formed the colony, subsequently the State, and gave up some of their powers to it; that new towns were settled and admitted to the union upon the same footing as were original towns, with all the rights, powers, and duties of the four original towns ; that little by little the power of the colony, afterwards the State, has increased and that of the towns has diminished; that this has been done with their consent; but among the rights still reserved to the towns and cities of this State are the right of existence and the right to manage their own local affairs, free from the interference or control of the general government except through the exercise of its undoubted power to pass general laws applicable to all alike.

The importance of the subject of the rights of our towns to the control of their own affairs, the increasing indifference or ignorance about them, and the continued assumption of illegal powers by the general assembly, in violation of the principles of Rhode

9

Island constitutional law, have required this lengthy examination of these rights.

The act creating a special board of canvassers and registration for the city of Providence only (G. L. cap. 8, sec. 22, amended, cap. 363); the act permitting the commissioner of public works in the city of Providence to employ a secretary (P. L. cap. 813); the act proposed for passage last spring directing the governor to appoint a board of police and license commissioners for the city of Providence, with extraordinary powers not only to administer the law but also to make it, to be paid large salaries by the city without being subject to its control ; and, lastly, the proposal for a special act by the general assembly to make the water bills of those occupying buildings in the city of Providence only, a lien upon the land of the owner (the user often not being the owner, and thus creating an obligation whereby one was to become bound, without his consent, to pay the debt of another)—all show the necessity of new constitutional restraints upon the further and continued encroachment by the general assembly upon the rights of our towns and cities to manage their own local affairs. This can only be done through a constitutional convention, and a constitutional convention we ought to have.

The requisites of a constitution should be borne in mind in attempting to frame a new one

It should contain, of course, a statement of the fundamentals of government. This includes an introduction, a declaration, or bill of rights (a statement of personal rights guaranteed to every one and inviolable by the government), a scheme of public management and administration (or division into the three co-ordinate departments, the legislative, the judicial, and the executive, with a statement of the powers of each and how exercised).

Then should follow articles relating to the electorate, to education, to the now important subject of corporations, their formation, powers, and duties, including municipal corporations, and how they may form and amend their own charters, including a mode for changing from town to city government. Other articles may be needed, or sections may be needed in some of the articles already enumerated, to introduce new safeguards or restrictions that experience has shown cannot be successfully carried into effect through ordinary legislation.

And lastly, so far as possible, mere legislation should not go into the constitution.

Let us pass in review some of the changes required to make the constitution what it should be in the light of the state of development of constitutional law of the present day.

There should be distinct recognition of the right of towns and cities to self-government. To make this effective it is necessary to provide, as do the constitutions of Missouri, California, and Washington, how towns and cities may make and alter their own charters by their own conventions, subject, of course, to the constitution and laws of the State. It is necessary also to provide that although the general assembly may pass general laws, no general laws shall interfere with the rights and powers of towns and cities incorporated according to law, nor shall any special law be passed affecting any town or city.

The experience in the three States named shows the scheme works well.

In 1876 the city of St. Louis framed its own charter in the manner suggested, through a convention of thirteen of its freeholders elected by its own voters, as authorized by the constitution of the State. This charter has been recognized generally by authorities on city government as the best American model for charter makers. (Oberholzer, The Referendum in America, 91.)

In Ewing v. Oblitzelle, 85 Mo. 64, it was held that there is no constitutional objection to allowing voters of a city to frame and adopt their own charter of government, if authorized by the State constitution to do so.

Kansas City, Mo., framed its own charter in the same way, in 1889, and the result proved to be satisfactory.

The measure having worked well in Missouri, when the constitutional convention of California met, in 1879, it was proposed to incorporate the same provision in the constitution. The politicians opposed it, professing great fear lest San Francisco, the only city in the State containing the requisite population of 100,000, would break loose from the rest of the State and set up a free government of its own.

" This is the boldest kind of an attempt at secession," said one speaker. The opposition was so great that the friends of the measure were compelled to accept an amendment that such a charter, accepted by the voters of the city, must be approved, also, by the legislature—to be approved or rejected as a whole, however, without power of alteration or amendment.

For years the active operation of the " city hall gang," a potent source of corruption in San Francisco, succeeded in defeating all charters drawn under this clause of the State constitution, but at last a majority voted to approve a charter thus framed by its own convention.

The scheme meeting with popular approval throughout the State, the constitution was amended to allow all cities of more than 10,000 inhabitants to frame their own charters. The second charter framed, by Los Angeles, under this power was approved by its voters and by the legislature, and is now in successful operation.

Oakland, Stockton, San Diego, and Sacramento have also framed their own charters, and they are now in effect and have proved successful.

The system working so well, by constitutional amendment in 1890 the right was extended to any city containing over 3,500 inhabitants.

In 1892, by constitutional amendment, it was provided that the charters thus framed and adopted shall become the organic law of the cities adopting them and shall supersede all laws inconsistent therewith, thus depriving the legislature of the power of interfering with them in any way by the passage even of general laws.

The constitution of Washington, of 1890, contains similar provisions. Those who fear the extension of this principle that the people can govern themselves, should read the debates in the convention and follow the subsequent history of this clause. Seattle has a charter thus framed, and the city comptroller writes that the "plan is acknowledged to be better than depending upon the legislature." Tacoma, in 1890, also adopted a charter of its own making. The mayor writes: "The new is felt to be superior to the old method."

Oberholzer concludes his examination of this subject:

"The interests of all our large cities are totally diverse from the interests of the remaining sections of the States in which they are placed by our artificial arrangement of boundaries. We have massed different peoples together who have no mutual sympathies, who are opposite in political and social standards, and antipodal in wants and governmental requirements. For the good of the cities themselves, and likewise for the good of the States, it is necessary that our large cities should be free cities."

An excellent commission has submitted lately a model charter for the city of Providence. Why should not its electors be allowed to decide upon its adoption? But even if adopted by the general assembly in the form recommended, what guarantee is there the general assembly will not change it at its own will, irrespective of the wishes of the citizens of Providence? Should not the possibility of such a course be removed by a constitutional inhibition? This can only be done through a constitutional convention.

The complex civilization of the present day, the increased power of a sometimes unscrupulous press, with facilities hitherto undreamt of for prying into men's private affairs and taking snap photographic portraits, renders it necessary to add to the bill of rights new safeguards guaranteeing the right to privacy of those who are not recognized public characters or engaged in public affairs. The extent of the necessity for such a safeguard can only be known to those who have examined the subject and have followed the many recent cases in the courts where private individuals have tried, too often unsuccessfully. to defend themselves or those dear to them from undue publicity. See the excellent article on the subject by Warren and Brandeis, IV Harvard Law Review, 193, where may be found the draft of a law to secure this recognition of the right to privacy. But it requires more than a law. It must find its appropriate place in the bill of rights.

Our English forefathers had laws against unjust imprisonment, but they were not enough until the habeas corpus act was passed and became accepted as a constitutional guarantee and in the United States was placed in our bill of rights.

We may not all agree as to what subjects the general assembly shall be forbidden to interfere with. Yet all must agree that there are such subjects. A glance at any of the recent State constitutions will show a concurrence in this idea and similarity in limiting the field of action of the State legislatures.

There would seem to be every reason why the old inhibition against the passage of *ex post facto* legislation should be made to include civil legislation as well as criminal legislation.

While the general assembly should have power to pass general laws affecting alike all towns and cities within specified classes, it should be deprived of power to interfere in the local affairs of any town or city.

The costs of suits where small sums are involved are so great that, in the interest of the large class of mechanics and others, wages or salaries of five hundred dollars a year, say ten dollars a week, should be exempt from attachment. (Personally the writer would thus exempt twenty dollars a week.)

Exemption of property from taxation when held for school, religious, or charitable purposes was well enough in the infancy of the colony, when there was little accumulated wealth. The necessity no longer exists. The time has come when the statement in Art. I, Sec. 2, " the burdens of the State ought to be fairly distributed among its citizens," should be made literally true. Of course we cannot take away the right to exemption from taxation if it has become vested. But we can and should prevent any further extension of the old doctrine.

Witnesses in criminal cases require more protection than they now have. The detention and imprisonment of such witnesses, in some instances, has worked great hardship. To say nothing of the injustice to them, it is bad public policy, because witnesses in criminal cases, fearing unjust detention, will avoid giving information, to escape summons, and thus crime is made more difficult of proof. This is no theoretical matter, but what actual experience proves.

The old mischievous theory that a claim against the State cannot be collected, because a judgment against the State cannot be be enforced, should be dropped. Every time that the State takes private property for public use, and pays for it what a jury awards, a claim against the State is enforced and collected. Why, then, should not other claims against the State be made matter for judicial cognizance ? It would be as logical to claim that all plans between nations for arbitration must fail because the award cannot be enforced. As a matter of fact, we know that arbitration works successfully. The United States has provided a court of claims in Washington, to entertain and decide suits by private parties against the United States, and the result is completely successful. It is time now to put the principle into the constitution of our State.

To guard against the public scandal and disgrace that have occurred in more than one State, it is necessary to prohibit allowance of any extra pay to any public officer. Massachusetts has sinned outrageously in this particular, and our general assembly is showing a tendency to follow in her footsteps. See the article on "Massachusetts as a Philanthropic Robber," by Charles Warren, in 12 Harvard Law Rev. 316.

As to the qualifications for the suffrage, they should be made as simple as possible. It is a mistake to have different classes of voters for different purposes. For it requires a complicated system of registration, makes fraud more easy, creates a system of caste

incompatible with American principles of government and be-
tokens a want of confidence in the democracy that we profess to
believe in. Upon comparison of States setting up different requisites, such as an educational qualification or the ownership of
property, real or personal, with other States without these prere-
quisites to suffrage, we find that however advantageous they may
be in theory, in practice they do not work according to the theory
that led to their adoption. The time has come when they should
be all swept away and the basis of suffrage be accepted as fixed
by the arrival at 21 years of age of every man and woman not disqualified through crime or mental incapacity. Coupled with this
the State should insist upon the education of all, to fit these voters
to protect the interests of the State, and included in such education should be the teaching, not of religion, but of the highest
morality, including political morality. We can only consider such
a desirable state reached when candidates aspiring to office cease
to offer bribes, directly or indirectly, and when voters ready to receive bribes can no longer be found.

This State has retained longer than any State in the Union its
property qualifications upon the exercise of the suffrage. Yet in
no respect do we find this State better governed than are other
States where there are no such restrictions. As a result of practical experience, therefore, no harm can come from their abolition,
and the time has come when we should carry into effect our pro-
fessed belief in a democratic form of government. It is safer to
to trust the whole of the people than any one section of it.

The extension of the suffrage to women is but a matter of time.
It is gaining ground everywhere and will reach us before long.
All the argument is in its favor, and there is nothing but conserva-
tism and sentiment to oppose it. It is the part of wisdom to
provide for the impending change in public opinion that will come
when women themselves want the suffrage. When they become
convinced of its wisdom, that it will benefit them as well as the
State, they will ask for it and they will get it. That it will benefit
the State to extend the suffrage to women follows from the fact
that no State is in a normal condition when any one large class of
its citizens is excluded from the suffrage. Consider, for instance,
the existing right of the husband to administer without accounta-
bility upon the personal estate of his wife dying intestate—a polite
method of designating his legal right to steal his deceased wife's
property. It is the last relic left of the old law, or want of law,

when, upon death of the owner of personal property, it became the property of the one that first seized it. Who can doubt that if women voted and took part as members of the general assembly in framing our laws the last vestige of this barbarous law would disappear?

It would be well, therefore, to make it possible for the general assembly to admit women to the suffrage when public opinion shall have rendered it feasible to take that course.

The great advantages gained in England by transferring all questions of contested elections to the determination of the judiciary should induce us to follow their example. When Thaddeus Stevens came into the national house of representatives one morning, asked what business was on and was told it was a contested election case, he said : " Well, which fellow is our damned rascal ? We will admit *him*." As the practice so frankly admitted is unquestioned, it is time the constitution should put a stop to its possibility.

The pay of the members should not be left open to the possibility of any " grab act " or " back pay act " nor should it be possible to distribute public offices among the members, as the " May Dealers " did in 1884.

The newly developing disposition to appoint public officers for towns and cities in the general assembly, who shall be paid by the towns and cities against their protest and without control over the officers thus appointed by the general assembly, should be checked by providing that all such officers appointed by the State shall be paid by the State. This can only be done by incorporating it into the constitution.

The tendency of the latest constitutions is to leave the formation of all corporations, even those having power to exercise of rights of eminent domain, to the operation of general laws to be framed by the legislature and to be construed by the judiciary. Public notice should be required of all applications for the exercise of this right ; no monopoly should be allowed for more than twenty years to any corporation, in return for the service to the public rendered and for adequate consideration only ; and the judiciary should be made the judge of what constitutes such contracts, monopolies, franchises, special privileges, and adequate consideration.

There can be no excuse for a bicameral legislature, if both chambers represent the same constituency. As a check upon the arbitrary exercise of power, different motives and considerations should influence the members of the two houses in concurring upon measures proposed. There is good reason for adhering to equal representation of every town and city in our senate. It is in accord with what is sought herein to be shown, the independent origin, the political supremacy, and the historical and constitutional development of these units of our political being. To correct the inequality of representation resulting therefrom, it is all the more imperative the representation in the lower house should be based upon population only, without regard to town lines. Therefore the State should be divided into districts, say one hundred or perhaps more in number, of equal population, as nearly as may be, each to elect one representative. Provision should also be made in this house for minority representation, in accordance with some plan easy of comprehension and application. This would be statesmanlike, practical, and effective.

Our State should no longer remain one of the three States in which the governor has no veto power, and that power should be given to him in such a form as to make it effective. The experience of other States has shown that he must be given power to veto severable parts of a bill instead of being given power to veto a bill only as a whole.

An independent judiciary, consisting of able, upright, learned judges, unbiased by political considerations or party affiliations, can be best secured by their appointment by that branch of the government that can be held the most directly responsible for the proper exercise of this power. As the executive is that branch, this power should be entrusted to him. The judges, once appointed, should be removable only because of old age or for good cause. That our present poor system has worked as well as it has is a tribute to the good sense and political capacity of our people, but is no reason for its continued existence.

How many years is it, however, since any man has been raised to the bench in Rhode Island unless he belonged to the dominant political party? It is time to inaugurate a system under which the best fitted men may be placed upon the bench, irrespective of the party to which they belong. This can only be done through a new constitution.

Of all the devices to promote honesty in the administration of public affairs and to prevent maladministration, experience shows that publicity is one of the most potent. For this reason all officers of the State should make public returns of all moneys received and spent in the discharge of their duties, and similar returns should be required of all handling money for election purposes or for the procuring or preventing the procuring of legislation, directly or indirectly. We have adopted a part of this system by requiring the publication of the accounts of all money received and paid by State officers. The experience of other States and of England proves that we must now extend this principle on the lines indicated.

The old inhibition of the grant of monopolies is now successfully evaded in the general assembly by coupling the illegal grant of the particular monopoly with some detriment to be incurred or consideration to be paid by the corporation or party to whom the grant is made. It matters not that the consideration paid is inadequate, for the grant has thereby become a contract. No matter how unjust or burdensome to the State, having thus become a contract through the cunning of the corporation lawyers, it cannot be amended or varied by the State except with the consent of the corporation, being protected by the United States constitution, (Art. 1, Sec. 10) which forbids any State from passing any law impairing the obligation of a contract.

This can only be prevented by a new clause in the bill of rights forbidding the making of such contracts by the general assembly except for adequate consideration and for a limited number of years only.

With publicity made requisite by law, and proper power vested somewhere to compel the giving of the requisite testimony concerning the management of public business, when a senator is accused by his colleague of the improper and illegal exercise of influence to procure funds for campaign purposes, the inquiry could not be successfully stifled, as we have witnessed in a neighboring New England State this summer.

It should be made possible to know whence comes the money, and how it is distributed, that keeps up legal protection over favored classes and individuals in this country and secures nomination and election to public office, often to the astonishment of the people, both in national and in state legislation, of the nominees of these interests.

The national committee of republicans and independents appointed by the independent conference, in New York, July 22, 1884, made its report at the close of the presidential campaign, setting forth in details the source of all its receipts for campaign purposes of $23,836.17, and every item of expenditure, amounting to $23,-408.33, leaving a balance on hand of $427.84. The account books, subscription lists, and vouchers were carefully examined and compared with the account submitted, by a competent auditing committee who certified the amount was correct and true.

This is what the constitution of the State should require in every political campaign. The above incident is particularly noteworthy as showing how it is practically possible to accomplish this, and therefore the law should require it.

It is acknowledged that organization in political matters is necessary, as it is in other matters. But organization in political matters is of public concern, and to secure honesty in political organizations we have a right to exact publicity. The political organization and its doings that require secrecy, require it to conceal wrong-doing.

It is always a mistake to commit the State to fixed periods only for revisions of the constitution. It is a denial of the right of the people to make and alter their constitution of government as necessity may demand. It is better to provide that the general assembly and the people, too, may suggest either amendments or a constitutional convention, as occasion may require. We have no right to make the rights of our successors any different from what our own rights are, with regard to the organic law of the State. Our forefathers had no right to limit our rights or to make them any different from what their own were over these matters. The principle always to be followed is the one expressly stated in Art. I, Sec. 1, and it is maintained herein that no limitation can be placed upon that principle—the right of the people, now and in all future time, to make and alter their constitution of government by the voice of the majority of the electors. A provision for a convention to revise the constitution at stated times, limits, by implication, the power to hold such a convention at any other time, and is, therefore, to be avoided. For the right of the people to make and alter their constitution of government is absolute, and therefore not be limited, expressly or by implication. This method has been tried in other States and found wanting. Why attempt, then, to introduce here what has proved to be faulty elsewhere?

With these considerations in mind, the following essay at a draft of such a constitution as Rhode Island ought to have is submitted to the people of this State :

DRAFT OF A NEW CONSTITUTION

STATE OF RHODE ISLAND.

WE, the people of the State of Rhode Island and Providence Plantations, grateful to Almighty God for the civil and religious liberty which He hath permitted us to establish and so long to enjoy, and looking to Him for a blessing upon our endeavors to secure and to transmit unimpaired to succeeding generations this precious inheritance, do ordain and establish this constitution of government. *Preamble.*

ARTICLE I.

Declaration of Certain Constitutional Rights and Principles.

In order to secure the religious and political freedom established by our revered ancestors and to preserve them for our posterity, we declare that the essential and unquestionable rights and principles hereinafter stated shall be strictly established, maintained and preserved, and shall be of paramount obligation in all legislative, judicial, and executive proceedings. *Declaration.*

SECTION 1. In the words of the Father of his Country, we declare that "the basis of our political systems is the right of the people to make and alter their constitutions of government; but that the constitution which at any time exists, till changed by an explicit and authentic act of the whole people, is sacredly obligatory upon all." *Rights of the people to make and alter their constitution.*

The electors of this State, including those who may be allowed to vote thereon, have therefore the inherent, sole, and exclusive right, by a majority of those voting thereon, to regulate their internal government and to alter, abolish, and reframe the constitution whenever they may deem it necessary : *Provided*, that such change be not repugnant to the constitution of the United States.

Objects of free governments. How laws should be made.

SEC. 2. All free governments are instituted for the protection, safety, and happiness of the people, through the equal enjoyment by all of life, liberty, and the rights of conscience. All laws therefore, shall be made for the good of the whole ; and the burdens of the State shall be fairly distributed among its citizens.

The constitution of the United States is the supreme law. Acknowledgment of the right of local self-government of the State and of the town or city.

SEC. 3. The constitution of the United States is the supreme law of the land. But the right of local self-government in the State is a constitutional right that the national government cannot infringe ; and the right of local self-government in the town or city is also a constitutional right that the State cannot infringe.

Religious freedom secured.

SEC. 4. Whereas, God has created the mind free and whereas, a principal object of our revered forefathers, in their settlement of this State, was *"to hold forth a lively experiment, that a flourishing civil State may stand and be best maintained with full liberty in religious concernments;"* we, therefore, declare that no man shall be compelled to frequent any church, nor to support any religion, religious worship, church, or ministry whatever, except in fulfillment of his own voluntary contract ; nor shall any man be enforced, restrained, molested, nor burdened in his body or goods ; nor disqualified from holding any office, nor any position of public trust ; nor from voting ; nor from serving on juries ; nor as a witness in any court of law ; nor rendered incompetent nor discredited as a witness ; on account of his religious belief or want of religious belief ; nor otherwise suffer in any manner whatsoever on account of his religious belief or want of religious belief ; and we therefore declare that every man shall be free to worship God, or to abstain from the worship of God, according to the dictates of his own conscience ; and to profess, and by argument to maintain, his opinion in matters of religion, and that the same shall in no wise diminish, enlarge or affect his civil capacity. All persons shall be alike protected in the peaceable and quiet enjoyment of their religious sentiments, convictions, and duties. No church, sect, denomination, nor religious belief shall be preferred over another, and no public money nor public property of any kind shall be used directly or indirectly in aid of any religious belief, church, sect, or religious institution: *Provided*, always, that nothing in this section contained shall ever excuse any act of licentiousness or justify any act inconsistent with the peace and safety of the State.

SEC. 5. Every person within this State ought to find a certain remedy, through recourse to the laws, for all injuries or wrongs which he may receive in his person, property, or character. He ought to obtain right and justice freely and without purchase, completely and without denial; promptly and without delay; conformably to the laws. *How the laws should be administered.*

SEC. 6. Legally, all men are born free and equal and have certain natural inherent and inalienable rights, among which are: the right to defend and freely enjoy their lives and liberties; to acquire, possess, protect, and enjoy property and reputation; to worship God according to the dictates of their individual conscience; to communicate freely their thoughts and opinions on all subjects (subject, however, to the law concerning slander and libel, and to responsibility for the abuse of that right); to assemble for their common good in a peaceable manner, to instruct their representatives and to apply to those invested with the powers of government for the redress of grievances or for other proper purposes, by petition, address, or remonstrance; to keep and bear arms in defence of themselves, their homes, and their property, or in aid of the civil power when thereto legally summoned (but subject to any law enacted by the general assembly to prevent the carrying of concealed weapons); the right to privacy, except when engaged in public service or in some public manner. *Individual rights secured.*

SEC. 7. The right of the people to be secure in their persons, papers, and possessions, against unreasonable searches and seizures shall not be violated; and no warrant shall issue, but on complaint in writing, upon probable cause, supported by oath or affirmation, and describing as nearly as may be the place to be searched and the persons or things to be seized. *Search warrants and seizures, not favored.*

SEC. 8. No person shall be held to answer for a crime which shall be punishable by death or by imprisonment in the State prison, unless on presentment or indictment by a *Provisions concerning criminal proceedings.*

grand jury, except in cases of impeachment, or in cases arising in the land or naval forces or in the militia when in actual service in time of war or public danger. No person shall be subject to be twice put in jeopardy for the same offence.

Bail, fines, and punishments not to be excessive.

SEC. 9. Excessive bail shall not be required, nor excessive fines imposed, nor cruel punishments inflicted; and all punishments shall be proportioned to the offence.

Bail and *habeas corpus.*

SEC. 10. All persons imprisoned shall be bailable by sufficient surety, unless for offences punishable by death or by imprisonment for life when the proof of guilt is evident or the presumption great. The privilege of the writ of *habeas corpus* shall not be suspended, unless in case of rebellion or invasion the public safety shall require it; nor ever, without the authority of the general assembly.

Rights of the accused.

SEC. 11. In all criminal prosecutions the accused shall enjoy the right to a speedy and public trial by an impartial jury; to be informed of the nature and cause of the accusation, to be confronted with the witnesses against him, to have compulsory process for obtaining them in his favor, to have the assistance of counsel in his defence, and shall be at liberty to speak for himself.

Rights of defendants in civil actions.

SEC. 12. No person shall remain imprisoned in any civil action after he shall have delivered up his property for the benefit of his creditors in the manner prescribed by law; nor shall any person be arrested nor imprisoned in any action based upon contract, unless he shall have committed some fraud or is about to abscond from or has absconded from the State; but the general assembly may secure the enforcement of a judgment at law or decree in equity by appropriate and adequate legislation.

What laws the general assembly may not pass.

SEC. 13. No laws shall be passed:

1, That are *ex post facto*, whether criminal or civil;

2, That impair the obligation of any contract;

3, That grant any irrevocable privilege, franchise, or immunity, except as hereinafter is specified;

4, That grant any special privilege or immunity to any one of a class which, upon the same terms, shall not be granted to all of that class;

5, Regulating the internal affairs of any town or city, except by general laws applicable to all of like class;

6, Establishing slavery or involuntary servitude, except as a punishment for crime, whereof the party shall have been duly convicted;

7, Allowing lotteries, games of chance, the sale of tickets in either, or gambling;

8, Subjecting to garnishment salaries or wages due for personal services under ten dollars per week, or at that rate;

9, Making any distinction between resident aliens and citizens in reference to the possession, enjoyment, or descent of property;

10, Exempting any property from taxation, or surrendering by any contract, grant, or otherwise the power to tax any property.

SEC. 14. No man shall be compelled to give evidence criminating himself; but he may testify in his own behalf, in which case he shall be deemed to have waived this exemption, and he shall then be subject to cross-examination. The omission to testify in his own behalf, however, shall not subject him to comment. *No one compelled to incriminate himself.*

SEC. 15. No one shall be deprived of life, liberty, or property, except by due process of law. *Life, liberty, and property protected.*

SEC. 16. No witness shall be unreasonably detained, nor confined in any building where criminals are imprisoned, nor shall he be detained for the purpose of securing his testimony longer than may be necessary to take his deposition. He shall be discharged upon giving sufficient security for his appearance at the trial. If unable to do so, his deposition shall be taken in the manner prescribed by law, and in the presence of the accused and his counsel, or without their presence if either or both shall fail to attend after reasonable notice of the time and place of the taking thereof. Any deposition authorized by this section shall be received as evidence at the trial, if the witness shall be dead, absent from the State, or physically unable to attend. *Protection of witnesses.*

SEC. 17. Every person shall be presumed innocent until he is pronounced guilty by the law; and no act of severity which is not necessary to secure an accused person shall be permitted. *Presumption of innocence: rights thereunder.*

SEC. 18. The right of trial by jury shall remain inviolate. The legislature may, by general law, provide for a change of *Trial by jury shall remain inviolate.*

11

venue, in case an impartial trial cannot be had in the county where the crime was committed.

Protection of private property. SEC. 19. Private property shall not be taken, damaged in value, nor destroyed for private use. It shall not be taken, damaged in value, nor destroyed for public use, without just compensation which must be paid before the taking. In all cases the necessity for the exercise of this power must be first determined by the supreme court and the amount of compensation must be determined by a jury in a manner to be determined by law, and the amount of compensation shall be determined without reference to any benefit that may be conferred **Fee of land taken for public use.** by betterment or otherwie. The fee of land taken for any public use shall remain vested in the owner thereof, his heirs and assigns, subject to the use for which the land was taken.

Rights of fishery. SEC. 20. The people of this State shall continue to enjoy and freely exercise all the rights of fishery and the privileges of the shore to which they have been heretofore entitled under the charter and usages of this State. But no new right is intended to be granted, nor any existing right impaired, by this declaration.

Military is subordinate: martial law not favored. SEC. 21. The military shall be held in strict subordination to the civil authority. And the law martial shall be used and exercised only in the army, navy, or militia in actual service in time of war or insurrection.

Quartering soldiers in house, forbidden, how far. SEC. 22. No soldier shall be quartered in any house, in time of peace, without the consent of the owner; nor, in time of war, but in a manner to be prescribed by law.

The truth a defence for libel, when. SEC. 23. In all trials for libel or slander, both civil and criminal, the truth, unless published or uttered from malicious motives, shall be sufficient defence to the persons charged.

Bribery forbidden. SEC. 24. Any person who shall, directly or indirectly, offer, give, or promise any money or thing of value, testimonial, privilege, or personal advantage to any executive or judicial officer, or member of the general assembly, candidate for any public office, or an elector, to influence him in the performance of any of his public or official duties, shall be guilty of bribery and shall be punished as shall be provided by law.

No State officer to take any fee. SEC. 25. No officer of the State nor member of the general assembly shall, directly or indirectly, receive any fee, nor be engaged as counsel, agent, or attorney in the prosecution of any claim or measure for or against the State, before the general assembly, under penalty of forfeiting his office upon conviction thereof in a court of justice.

SEC. 26. The general assembly shall not: Restrictions upon general assembly.

1, Grant or confer any hereditary emolument, privilege, title, or power;

2, Attaint any person of treason or felony ;

3, Make any distinction in social status between any inhabitants of this State.

SEC. 27. Treason against the State shall consist only in Treason. levying war against it, or in adhering to its enemies and giving them aid and comfort. No person shall be convicted of treason, except upon the testimony of at least two witnesses to the same overt act, or upon confession in open court. No conviction of treason or other crime shall work corruption of blood nor forfeiture of estate, except during the life of the person convicted.

SEC. 28. Nothing shall at any time be allowed to interfere Suffrage to be inviolate. with nor prevent the free, full, and lawful exercise of the privilege of suffrage.

SEC. 29. All persons resident in this State, citizens of the Who are citizens. United States, are hereby declared to be citizens of this State.

SEC. 30. The legislature may, by general law, provide a Claims against the State. method by which citizens may prosecute claims against the State.

SEC. 31. The provisions of this constitution are mandatory Constitution is mandatory and prohibitory, unless declared to be otherwise by express and prohibitory. words.

SEC. 32. Monopolies are contrary to the genius of a free Monopolies prohibited. people and shall not be granted, except as herein is provided.

SEC. 33. No extra compensation shall be made to any No extra pay to any public officer, committeeman, commissioner, servant, or employé, agent, or contractor of the State, town, or city, after officer, &c. services shall have been rendered or contract made.

SEC. 34. No grant of exclusive, separate public emolument Charters, &c., subject to or privileges shall be made to any man or set of men, nor to revocation or amendment. anyone, except in consideration of public services; and every grant of a franchise, charter, privilege, or exemption shall remain subject to revocation, alteration, or amendment.

SEC. 35. The enumeration of the foregoing rights shall Rule of construction. not be construed to impair or deny others retained by the people.

Article II.

Of Qualifications of Electors.

Qualifications of electors.

Section 1. Every male inhabitant of this State, of the age of twenty-one years, who has been a citizen of the United States for ninety days, who has had his residence and home in this State for one year and in the town or city in which he may claim a right to vote six months next preceding the time of voting, and who shall have been duly registered as provided by law, shall have a right to vote in all elections of civil officers by the people, and on all questions in all legal town, ward, or district meetings.

Who shall not be permitted to vote.

Sec. 2. No idiot, insane person, pauper, or person under guardianship, or person *non compos mentis* shall be permitted to vote; nor shall any person convicted of either giving or receiving any bribe for voting, or convicted of any crime and punished therefor by imprisonment in the State prison, be permitted to be registered nor to vote until the general assembly shall, by special act, restore the right. The general

When right to vote may be declared forfeited.

assembly may impose a forfeiture of the right to vote in punishment of offences against the fairness or freedom of elections, and may, by special act, restore the right.

Who shall not gain residence.

Sec. 3. No person in the military, naval, marine, or any other service of the United States shall be considered as having the required residence by reason of being employed in any garrison, barrack, or military or naval station in this state, nor by reason of residing upon lands ceded to the United States.

Electors absent from the state in the military service of the United States, allowed to vote.

Sec. 4. Electors of this State who in time of war are absent from the state, in the actual military service of the United States, being otherwise qualified, shall have a right to vote in all elections in the State for electors of president and vice-president of the United States, representatives in congress, and general officers of the State. The general assembly shall have full power to provide by law for carrying this article into effect.

Powers of general assembly as to elections.

Sec. 5. The general assembly shall provide for a registry of voters, and for canvassing the voting lists; prescribe the nature of the evidence to be required as to the right of any person to vote, the manner of conducting elections, the counting of the votes, the authentication of the results, and shall enact all laws necessary to carry this article into effect and to prevent abuse, corruption, bribery, and fraud in elections.

SEC. 6. The general assembly may, by general law, extend the suffrage to women at any election of school officers or upon any measure relating to schools, upon the same qualifications as to men. But such law shall take effect only upon its passage by the succeeding general assembly. *Suffrage on school matters may be extended to women by general assembly.*

SEC. 7. The general assembly may extend the suffrage to women upon the same qualifications as to men, but such law shall take effect only upon its passage by the succeeding general assembly. *Suffrage may be extended to women by general assembly.*

SEC. 8. That the will of the people of the State may be enforced and the right of representation in the general assembly by the duly elected representative of the electors may be preserved, all cases of contested election shall be decided by the judiciary before the next regular session of the general assembly. The general assembly shall carry this provision into effect by appropriate legislation. *Contested elections to be determined by the courts.*

ARTICLE III.

Of the Distribution of Powers.

The powers of the government shall be distributed into three departments: the legislative, the executive, and the judicial. *Three departments of government.*

ARTICLE IV.

Of the Legislative Power.

SECTION 1. Subject to the constitution of the United States and the laws passed thereunder by the congress of the United States, this constitution shall by the supreme law of the State, and any law inconsistent therewith shall be void. The general assembly shall enact all laws necessary to carry this constitution into effect. *This constitution is the supreme law.*

SEC. 2. The legislative power under this constitution shall be vested in a general assembly which shall consist of two houses, one to be called the senate, and the other the house of representatives. The concurrence of the two houses, each acting in its own chamber, shall be necessary to the enactment *General assembly.*

Enacting style
of laws.
of laws. The enacting clause of all laws shall be, *It is enacted by the General Assembly as follows :*

Session of gen-
eral assembly.
SEC. 3. There shall be a session of the general assembly at Providence, commencing on the first Tuesday of January in each year.

Members ex-
empted from
arrest, and
privileged in
debate.
SEC. 4. The person of every member of the general assembly shall be exempt from arrest in any civil action during any session of the general assembly and for the two days next before and the two days next after any session, and all process served contrary hereto shall be void. For any speech in debate, in either house or in grand committee, no member shall be questioned in any other place.

Quorum.
SEC. 5. A majority of either house shall be a quorum to
Powers of less
than a quorum.
do business therein ; but a smaller number may adjourn from day to day and may compel the attendance of absent members in such manner, and under such penalties, as may be prescribed by the rules of the house compelling attendance, or by law. The organization of the two houses may be regulated by law, subject to the limitations contained in this constitution.

Rules of pro-
cedure ; pun-
ishments for
contempts ;
punishment
and expulsion
of members.
SEC.' 6. Each house may determine its rules of proceeding, punish contempts, punish its members for disorderly behavior, and, with the concurrence of two-thirds, expel a member; but not a second time for the same cause.

Journal to be
kept ; yeas and
nays, when to
be entered.
SEC. 7. Each house shall keep a journal of its proceedings. The yeas and nays of the members of either house shall be entered on the journal at the request of three members in the senate; or of five members in the house.

Adjournment
of general as-
sembly.
SEC. 8. Neither house, without the consent of the other, shall adjourn for more than four days, nor to any other place than that in which they may be sitting.

Pay of mem-
bers.
SEC. 9. The members of the general assembly shall receive compensation for their services and for actual traveling expenses paid by them by general law. But their pay shall not be increased nor diminished during the term for which they are elected.

Compensation
of officers.
SEC. 10. The general assembly shall regulate the compensation of the governor, and of all other State officers, which shall be paid by the State, subject to the limitations contained in this constitution.

All officers to
continue in
SEC. 11. All officers of annual or longer term of election

or appointment shall continue in office until other persons are qualified to take their places. office until successors are qualified.

SEC. 12. All lotteries shall be prohibited in this State. Lotteries prohibited.

SEC. 13. The general assembly shall have no power hereafter, without the express consent of the people, to incur State debts to an amount exceeding in the aggregate, at any one time, one hundred thousand dollars, except in time of war, or in case of insurrection or invasion; nor shall it in any case, without such consent, pledge the faith of the State for the payment of the obligations of others. State debts not to be incurred without consent of people, except in what cases.

SEC. 14. The assent of four-fifths of the members elected to each house of the general assembly shall be required to every bill appropriating the public money or property for local or private purposes. Private or local appropriations require a four-fifths vote.

SEC. 15. The general assembly shall, at least once in ten years, provide for making new valuations of property throughout the State, as a basis for the assessment of taxes. Valuations of property for purposes of taxation, when to be taken.

SEC. 16. The general assembly shall also provide by law for the annual revision of the list of electors in every town and city in the State. List of electors to be revised annually.

SEC. 17. No corporation shall be created with the power to exercise the right of eminent domain, or to acquire franchises in the streets and highways of towns and cities, except by general laws provided for that purpose that shall also provide for public notice of the proposal or intention to exercise said powers. Certain corporations to be created only by act of general assembly. Notice of pendency of petition to be given.

SEC. 18. The general assembly shall provide by general law for the creation and control of other corporations and the amendments of their charters. The general assembly shall not create any municipal corporation. General assembly to provide by general law for creation of other corporations, but cannot create any municipal corporation.

SEC. 19. The general assembly shall not adopt any measure the effect of which shall be that the State enters into, or becomes a party to, any contract granting directly or indirectly any monopoly, franchise, or special privilege for more than twenty years nor without adequate consideration. The supreme court shall be the judge of what constitutes such a contract, monopoly, franchise, special privilege, and adequate consideration.

SEC. 20. It shall be the duty of the two houses, upon the request of either, to join in grand committee for elections, at such times and in such manner as may be prescribed by law. Two houses shall join in grand committee for elections.

SEC. 21. The grand committee shall consist of the members of the senate and house of representatives sitting together, after having assembled pursuant to the vote of both houses. The method of its organization and of conducting elections therein shall be such as is or may prescribed by law, subject to the provisions of this constitution. A majority of the members elected to each house of the general assembly shall be necessary to constitute a quorum of the grand committee.

SEC. 22. The general assembly shall not authorize any city, town, or incorporated district to guarantee the indebtedness of any corporation, association, institution, or individual.

SEC. 23. No act, or section thereof, shall be revived or amended by reference to its title only; but the act or section, as revived or amended, shall be enacted and set forth in full.

SEC. 24. No district with general town powers without town representation shall be established.

SEC. 25. No law can be passed, except by bill. Bills may originate in either house of the general assembly, but they may be amended, altered, or rejected in the other house. No law shall relate to more than one subject, and that shall be expressed in the title. Each law shall recite at length the provisions enacted and shall take effect upon the rising of the general assembly, unless an earlier date is provided in the act. No bill shall be considered for passage, unless it has first been referred to a committee and reported therefrom at least three days before the final adjournment of the general assembly. Every bill, before passage, must be read by sections or by title on three different days and must have been read at length on its final passage, in each house of the general assembly. No bill shall become a law, unless, on its final passage, it receives in each house the vote of a majority of the members elected to that house. The supreme court shall have power to declare any act, or part of an act, unconstitutional and void not passed in compliance with the provisions of this section.

SEC. 26. The general assembly shall not pass any local or special law for the following purposes:

1, Changing the names of any person ;

2, Adopting any person ;

3, Declaring any person of age ;

Marginal notes:

Grand committee, how constituted.

Organization of, and method of conducting elections in.

Quorum.

Cities and towns not to guarantee indebtedness of corporations, etc.

Acts revived or amended, form of.

No district without town powers to be established

All laws to be by bill, and requisites of passage.

What local or special laws prohibited.

4, Granting divorces;

5, Granting to any person or corporation any monopoly, exclusive privilege, immunity, or franchise, except as herein provided ;

6, Granting to any person or corporation the right to lay down railroad tracks, except on land belonging to the State, unless under the exercise of the power of eminent domain ;

7, Remitting fines, penalties, or forfeitures ;

8, Providing for the bonding of cities, towns or other municipalities ;

9, Regulating town or city affairs ;

10, Regulating the election of town or city officers ;

11, Regulating the fees or salary of any town or city officer;

12, Creating or prescribing the powers and duties of town and city officers ;

13, Exempting property from taxation ;

14, Creating any corporation or amending any charter.

SEC. 27. No local or special bill shall be passed unless notice of the intention to apply therefor shall have been published in the locality where the matter or thing to be effected is situated, which notice shall be at least thirty days prior to the introduction into the general assembly of such bill and in the manner to be provided by law; the evidence of such notice having been published shall be exhibited in the general assembly before such act shall be passed. *Notice to be given of pendency of local or special bill.*

SEC. 28. The general assembly may, by general law, provide for the borrowing of money by bond or otherwise by the towns and cities in the State, but the amount so borrowed shall never, at any time, exceed ten per centum upon the State valuation of the value of the property in any town or city. *General assembly may authorize towns and cities to issue bonds not to exceed ten per centum on State valuation.*

SEC. 29. All general laws or laws of a public nature must be uniform throughout the State.

SEC. 30. The general assembly shall continue to exercise the powers they have heretofore exercised, unless prohibited in this constitution. *General assembly to exercise its former powers unless prohibited herein.*

ARTICLE V.

Of the House of Representatives.

House of representatives, how constituted.
SECTION 1. The house of representatives shall consist of one hundred members, and shall be constituted on the basis of population, always allowing one representative for a fraction exceeding one half the ratio. The State shall be divided into one hundred districts. The present ratio shall be one representative to every 3,847 inhabitants, and the general assembly shall, after any new census taken by the authority of the United States or of this State, re-apportion the representation by altering the ratio. The one hundred districts shall be divided into ten groups, of ten adjacent districts each, at such re-apportionment. In each group the names of the candidates to the house in the ten districts shall be placed on one ticket, and each voter within the group shall vote for six representatives. The ten representatives receiving the largest number of votes in each group shall be declared elected.

May elect its officers.

Precedence of Newport members at organization.
SEC. 2. The house of representatives shall have authority to elect its speaker, clerks, and other officers. The senior in age of the members elect from the city of Newport, present at the time, shall preside in the organization of the house.

ARTICLE VI.

Of the Senate.

Senate, how constituted.
SECTION 1. The senate shall consist of the lieutenant-governor and of one senator from each town and city.

Presiding officer, and his right to vote.
SEC. 2. The lieutenant-governor shall preside in the senate and in grand committee, with the right to vote in case of an equal division, but not in elections.

Shall choose a president of the senate, when.
The senate shall choose a president to preside when the lieutenant-governor is absent, or when he shall refuse to act as president, or shall act as governor, or when the office of lieutenant-governor is vacant.

Secretary of State to be secretary of senate.
SEC. 3. The secretary of state, by virtue of his office, shall be secretary of the senate, and secretary of the grand committee unless otherwise provided by law.

SEC. 4. The senate shall have authority to elect its own clerks and such other officers as it may deem necessary.

May elect its own clerks, &c.

ARTICLE VII.

Of the Executive Power.

SECTION 1. The chief executive power of this State shall be vested in a governor, who, together with a lieutenant-governor, shall be elected by the people.

Governor to be chief executive officer.

SEC. 2. The governor shall take care that the laws be faithfully executed.

To execute the laws.

SEC. 3. He shall be captain-general and commander-in-chief of the military and naval forces of this State, except when they shall be called into the service of the United States.

To be commander-in-chief.

SEC. 4. He shall have power to grant reprieves after conviction, except in cases of impeachment, for not longer than thirty days after the beginning of the next session of the general assembly.

Governor may grant temporary reprieves.

SEC. 5. The governor, with the approval in writing of the judges of the supreme court, or of a majority of their number, after the examination by both of the record in each case, shall have power for good cause to grant pardons after conviction. The governor shall submit a statement in writing to the general assembly in each case, setting forth the reasons why he has granted a pardon.

Governor may grant pardons, and how.

SEC. 6. He may fill vacancies in office not otherwise provided for by this constitution or by law, until the same shall be filled by the general assembly or by the people.

May fill vacancies temporarily.

SEC. 7. Every bill passed by the legislature shall be presented to the governor before it becomes a law, and if he approve it, he shall sign it. He may veto any bill by returning it with his objections to the house in which it originated. If passed over his veto by a vote of three-fifths of the members of each house, entered on the journal, it shall become a law. If a bill be kept ten days, Sundays excepted, by the governor without returning it, after it shall have been presented to him. it shall become law without his approval; but if the legislature adjourn during the said ten days, no such bill shall become a law without the approval of the governor.

Veto power.

No bill shall become a law after the final adjournment of the general assembly, unless approved by the governor within thirty days after such adjournment. The governor shall have power to veto any specific items in any bill appropriating money. He shall also have power to veto severable parts of a bill that relate to different subjects. In such case he shall append to the bill at the time of signing it a statement of the items or subjects to which he objects, and his reasons therefor, and the items or subjects objected to shall be separately reconsidered and shall not become law, unless passed over his veto by a vote of three-fifths of each house entered on the journal.

May adjourn assembly, when.

SEC 8. In case of disagreement between the two houses of the general assembly respecting the time or place of adjournment, certified to him by either, he may adjourn them to such time and place as he shall think proper: *Provided*, that the time of adjournment shall not be extended beyond the day of the next stated session.

May convene assembly, when.

SEC. 9. He may, on extraordinary occasions, convene the general assembly at any town or city in this State, at any time not provided for by law; and in case of danger from the prevalence of epidemic or contagious disease in the place in which the general assembly is by law to meet, or to which it may have been adjourned, or for other urgent reasons, he may by proclamation convene said assembly at any other place within this State.

Commissions, style of, and by whom signed.

SEC. 10. All commissions shall be in the name and by authority of the State of Rhode Island and Providence Plantations; shall be sealed with the State seal, signed by the governor, and attested by the secretary of State.

Lieutenant-governor shall act as governor, when.

SEC. 11. In case of the death, resignation, removal from the State, impeachment and conviction of the governor, or of vacancy in the office from any cause, the lieutenant-governor shall be the governor; and in case of the inability of the governor to serve, or of his absence from the State, the lieutenant-governor shall be acting governor during such inability or absence.

President of the senate shall act as governor, when.

SEC. 12. If the offices of governor and lieutenant-governor be both vacant, by reason of death or otherwise, the president of the senate shall be acting governor until such offices are filled by the general assembly; and in case of the temporary absence from the State of the governor and lieutenant-governor, or of the inability of both of them to serve, the president of the senate shall be the acting governor during such inability or absence. Whenever the president of the senate shall act as governor or lieutenant-governor, he shall be entitled only to his vote as senator on any question or election in the senate or grand committee.

SEC. 13. The compensation of the governor and lieutenant-governor shall be established by law, and shall not be diminished during the term for which they are elected.

Compensation of the governor and lieutenant-governor.

SEC. 14. There shall be a secretary of State, an attorney-general, and a general treasurer, whose powers and duties shall be such as may be prescribed by law. The general assembly shall provide by law for annual reports from each of said officers as to the business in his department, and the report of the attorney-general shall include the disposition of cases in which the State is interested.

Duties and powers of the other general officers.

ARTICLE VIII.

Of the Judicial Power.

SECTION 1. The judicial power of this State shall be vested in a court of common pleas, a superior court, a supreme court, and such inferior courts as the general assembly may from time to time ordain and establish.

Judicial power, where vested.

SEC. 2. The court of common pleas shall have original jurisdiction in all jury cases, whether civil or criminal. It shall have appellate jurisdiction, in manner to be provided by law, in all civil cases from inferior courts in which the debt or damages laid in the writ shall exceed three hundred dollars; of all crimes, offences, and misdemeanors brought before it by appeal, commitment, recognizance, indictment, or otherwise; and of such cases from inferior courts as the general assembly may by law determine. The justices of this court shall instruct the jury in the law in all trials.

Jurisdiction of court of common pleas.

SEC. 3. The superior court shall have original jurisdiction in all suits and proceedings in equity, petitions for mechanics liens, and other statutory proceedings following the course of equity, with power to make and enforce all orders and decrees therein, and to issue all process therefor, according to the

Jurisdiction of superior court.

94

course of equity ; of petitions for new trials, divorce, separate maintenance, alimony, and custody of children. It shall have exclusive authority to issue writs of error, certiorari, mandamus, prohibition, and quo warranto ; and to entertain informations in the nature of a writ of quo warranto, and of writs of habeas corpus ; and may issue all other extraordinary writs and processes to courts of inferior jurisdiction, corporations, societies, associations, copartnership, and individuals that may be necessary for the furtherance of justice and for the due administration of the laws ; with all incidental powers necessary to the proper discharge of its duties according to law.

Jurisdiction of supreme court. SEC. 4. The supreme court shall have jurisdiction in the review of all questions of law and of equity, upon appeal from the lower courts.

General assembly may confer additional jurisdiction. SEC. 5. Each of these three courts shall have such additional and appellate jurisdiction as may be conferred upon. it by the general assembly.

Judges, how appointed, &c. SEC. 6. The justices of the court of common pleas, of the superior court, and of the supreme court shall be appointed by the governor, from members of the bar learned in the law and distinguished for their high attainments and character, irrespective of party, but not more than a majority of any one of said courts shall be members of the same political party. Each justice shall hold his office during good behavior, until he reaches the age of seventy years, but any justice may be re-appointed by the governor from year to year, after reaching the age of seventy years. But a justice of any court shall be removed from office if, upon impeachment, he shall be found guilty of any official misdemeanor.

Vacancy, how filled. SEC. 7. In case of vacancy by death, resignation, removal from the State or from office, refusal or inability to serve of any justice of the court of common pleas, superior court or supreme court, the governor shall appoint his successor. In case of impeachment or temporary absence or temporary inability, the governor may appoint a person to discharge the duties of the office during the vacancy caused thereby. He shall also be removed from office by the governor, assisted in his judgment therein by the *ex-officio* members of the supreme and superior court at that time retired on pension, if any there be, for any gross misbehavior incompatible with the dignity of his office, upon complaint made, stating the cause for which such removal is deemed necessary. He shall be given an opportunity to be heard thereon, and to be represented by counsel if he so desire, and he shall be served with a copy of said complaint at least twenty days before such hearing. The governor shall state in writing his reasons for any removal made under this section.

SEC. 8. The justices of said court shall receive compensation for their services, and provision for their old age, by way of pension after retirement, as the general assembly may by law determine, which, however, shall not be diminished during their continuance in office. *Compensation of judges.*

SEC. 9. The cities and towns of the State may elect such justices of the peace or wardens resident therein as they may deem proper, and the towns of New Shoreham and Jamestown may continue to elect their wardens as heretofore, whose jurisdiction shall be regulated by law, and who shall be commissioned by the governor. *Justices of the peace. Wardens for New Shoreham and Jamestown.*

SEC. 10. The justices of the supreme court shall give their written opinion upon any question of law whenever requested by the governor or by either house of the general assembly : *Provided*, that they may decline to answer such questions as in their opinion they cannot properly decide, and no such opinion shall be deemed to be a judicial determination. *Duties of justices of supreme court.*

SEC. 11. The judges of the several courts shall, in all jury trials before them, instruct the jury in the law. *Same subject.*

ARTICLE IX.

Of Elections.

SECTION 1. The governor, lieutenant-governor, senators, representatives, secretary of State, attorney general, general treasurer and senators and representatives in the general assembly shall be elected by ballot in the manner now or hereafter required by law, at the town, city, ward, or district meetings, to be holden on the Wednesday next after the first Monday in December in each year, and shall severally hold their offices for one year from the first Tuesday of January next succeeding their election, and until their successors are elected and duly qualified to fill their places. *General officers and members of general assembly, when elected, and tenure of office.*

Votes for general officers, how taken and to be treated.

SEC. 2. The names of the persons voted for as governor, lieutenant-governor, secretary of State, attorney general, and general treasurer shall be placed upon one ticket; and all votes for these officers shall, in open town or ward meetings, be sealed up by the moderators and town clerks and by the wardens and ward clerks, who shall certify the same and deliver or send them to the secretary of State; whose duty it shall be securely to keep and deliver the same to the grand committee after the organization of the two houses at the next session.

Power of general assembly over list of voters, &c.

SEC. 3. The general assembly shall have power to pass general laws concerning a list or register of all persons qualified to vote for general officers, senators, and representatives, the counting of the ballots, the announcement of the result, the giving of certificates to the officers elected and the ordering of new elections.

Lieutenant-governor elect shall be qualified as governor, when.

General officers to be elected by general assembly in grand committee, when.

SEC. 4. When the governor elect shall die, remove from the State, refuse to serve, become insane, or be otherwise incapacitated, the lieutenant-governor elect shall be qualified as governor at the beginning of the term for which he was elected. When both the governor and lieutenant-governor elect, or either the lieutenant-governor, secretary of State, attorney-general, or general treasurer elect are so incapacitated, or when there has been a failure to elect any one or more of the officers mentioned in this section, the general assembly shall upon its organization meet in grand committee and elect some person or persons to fill the office or offices, as the case may be, for which such incapacity exists, or as to which such failure to elect occurred. When the general assembly shall elect any of said officers because of the failure of any person to receive a plurality of the votes cast, the election in each case shall be made from the persons who received the same and largest number of votes.

When offices of governor and lieutenant-governor be both vacant, how to be filled.

Duty of acting governor in such an event.

SEC. 5. If the offices of governor and lieutenant-governor be both vacant, by reason of death or otherwise, they shall be filled by the general assembly in grand committee, and the acting governor shall, if the general assembly is not then in session, call a special session thereof for that purpose within twenty days after both of said offices become vacant, if a stated session is not sooner to occur.

SEC. 6. In case of a vacancy in the office of secretary of

State, attorney-general, or general treasurer, from any cause, the general assembly in grand committee shall elect some person to fill the same : *Provided*, that if such vacancy occurs when the general assembly is not in session the governor shall appoint some person to fill such vacancy until a successor elected by the general assembly is qualified to act. Vacancy in offices of secretary of State, attorney-general, or general treasurer, how filled.

SEC. 7. When a senator or representative elect shall die, remove from the State, refuse to serve, become insane, or be otherwise incapacitated, or when at an election for any senator or representative no person shall receive a plurality of the votes cast, a new election shall be held. A vacancy in the senate or house of representatives shall be filled at a new election. The general assembly shall provide by general law for the holding of such elections at such times as to insure that each town and city shall be fully represented in the general assembly during the whole of every session thereof, so far as is practicable. Every person elected in accordance with this section shall hold his office for the remainder of the term or for the full term, as the case may be, of the office which he is elected to fill, and until his successor is elected and qualified. Vacancy in general assembly, how filled.

SEC. 8. In elections by the general assembly in grand committee the person receiving a majority of the votes shall be elected. Every person elected by the general assembly to fill a vacancy, or pursuant to section 2 of this article, shall hold his office for the remainder of the term or for the full term, as the case may be, and until his successor is elected and qualified. In elections by general assembly, majority to elect.

Tenure of office of persons elected by.

SEC. 9. Elections by the people shall be conducted in the manner now prescribed by law, until otherwise provided by the general assembly, subject to the provisions of this constitution. Elections by people, how to be conducted.

SEC. 10. In all elections by the people the person receiving a plurality of the votes cast shall be elected. In elections by the people plurality to elect.

SEC. 11. The general assembly shall provide by law for the trial and determination of all contested elections in the courts. Contested elections.

ARTICLE X.

Of Qualifications for Office.

Qualified electors only eligible.

SECTION 1. No person shall be elected by the people to any civil office (except the office of school committee) unless he is a qualified elector for such office.

Conviction of bribery a disqualification.

SEC. 2. Every person shall be disqualified from holding any office to which he may have been elected, upon conviction of having offered, or procured any other person to offer, any bribe to secure his election or the election of any other person.

General officers, how engaged.

SEC. 3. All general officers shall take the following engagement before they act in their respective offices, to wit: You ⸻ having been by the free vote of the electors of this State of Rhode Island and Providence Plantations elected unto the place of ⸻ do solemnly swear (or affirm) to be true and faithful unto this State, and to support the constitution of the United States and of this State; that you will faithfully and impartially discharge all the duties of your aforesaid office to the best of your abilities, according to law: So help you God. Or, this affirmation you make and give upon the peril of the penalty of perjury.

Members of assembly, the judges, and all other officers, how engaged.

SEC. 4. The members of the general assembly, the judges of all the courts, and all other officers, both civil and military, shall be bound by oath or affirmation to support the constitution of the United States and of this State.

By whom the general officers and members of assembly shall be engaged.

SEC. 5. The governor, lieutenant-governor, senators, and representatives shall be engaged by the secretary of State, or by a justice of the supreme court. The secretary of State, attorney-general, and general treasurer shall be engaged by the governor, or by a justice of the supreme court.

General officers and members of assembly not to hold certain offices.

SEC. 6. No person shall act as a general officer or as a member of the general assembly, who, at the time of taking or while occupying such office, shall hold any office made by law incompatible therewith; nor shall any person be elected to any office within the gift of the general assembly while a member thereof nor during the term he was elected to fill.

All persons elected to public office, to make return of all money, &c., spent, &c.

SEC. 7. To the end that the people may be protected in their political rights and because publicity tends to preserve those rights, by the prevention of fraud, every person elected to public office shall make a true and correct statement under oath or affirmation according to the best of his knowledge, information, and belief, specifying what is stated of his own knowledge and what is stated upon information and belief, within thirty days after his election, to the secretary of State for publication thereof, of all money or other consideration paid, offered, promised, given, or delivered or to be paid, offered, promised, given, or delivered, by or for him, directly or indirectly, in connection with his election.

SEC. 8. A like statement shall be made within thirty days after the adjournment of the general assembly to the secretary of State, for publication, by every one, whether a person, persons, association, club, company, corporation, copartnership, committee, or however, otherwise, handling or controlling campaign funds or money or other consideration for election purpose during all elections in the preceding year, of all such money or other consideration received and paid, or to be received or paid for such purposes, and the details or items of such statements shall be audited and verified as the general assembly shall by law provide. *All persons handling, &c., money, &c., for election or campaign purposes, to make return thereof.*

SEC. 9. Every one, whether a person, persons, association, club, company, corporation, copartnership, committee, or however otherwise petitioning or causing the general assembly to be petitioned for the passage of any measure, or appearing, or causing any one to appear, before any committee of either house of the general assembly, in support of, or in opposition to any measure pending before the general assembly for money or other consideration, shall ·make a like statement to the secretary of State for publication, within thirty days after the adjournment of each session of the general assembly, of all money or other consideration paid, offered, promised, given, delivered or received, or to be paid, offered, promised, given, delivered or received, whether directly or indirectly, for services rendered or to be rendered in connection therewith. *All persons petitioning the general assembly, to make return of money, &c., paid, &c.*

The general assembly shall carry the provisions of sections 7, 8, and 9 into effect by appropriate legislation that shall provide adequate remedies for punishing all violations thereof and effectual means for the enforcement thereof.

ARTICLE XI.

Of Impeachments.

Who liable to impeachment. SECTION 1. The governor and all executive and judicial officers shall be liable to impeachment for treason, bribery, or other crimes and misdemeanors, or for misconduct in office; but judgment in such cases shall not extend further Effect of conviction. than to removal from office. The person impeached, whether convicted or acquitted, shall, nevertheless, be liable to prosecution and punishment otherwise, according to law.

Impeachments, how to be ordered. SEC. 2. The house of representatives shall have the sole power of impeachment. A vote of two-thirds of all the members elected shall be required for the impeachment of the governor, and·for the impeachment of any other officer a vote of a majority of all the members elected shall be required. No judicial officer, nor officer having custody of public funds, shall exercise his office after impeachment, until he has been acquitted.

Impeachments, how to be tried. SEC. 3. The senate shall try all impeachments, and when sitting for that purpose the members thereof shall be under oath or affirmation to give the accused an impartial trial. No person shall be convicted except by vote of two-thirds of the members elected. When the governor is impeached the chief or presiding justice of the supreme court shall preside, with a casting vote in all preliminary questions.

ARTICLE XII.

Of City Charters.

How a city may revise its charter, or a town may become a city. SECTION 1. The electors of any city desirous of revising its charter, or of any town desirous of becoming a city, may revise its charter or frame its charter, all such charters to be subject to this constitution. For this purpose they may cause a convention to be called, to be composed of fifteen persons who shall be electors at least five years in such city or town and who shall be elected at an election to be held for such purpose in such city or town. It shall be the duty of the members of such convention to meet, to prepare and to propose the revised charter for such city, or a charter for such town desirous of becoming a city. Said charter shall be signed in duplicate by the members of such convention or a majority of them, and they shall return one copy thereof to the mayor of said city or to the president of the town council of said town and the other to the recorder of deeds of said city or town. After publication thereof, as said city or town council shall order and within not less than thirty days nor more than sixty days thereafter, such charter shall be submitted to the vote of the electors of said city or town at a general or special election. If ratified by a majority of the electors voting thereon, it shall be submitted to the general assembly for its approval or rejection as a whole; and if approved by the general assembly, it shall become the charter of such city, or town desirous of becoming a city, shall become the organic law thereof, and shall supersede any existing charter or law inconsistent therewith. Copies thereof certified by the mayor of said city, setting forth the submission of said charter to the electors and its ratification by them, shall be made in duplicate and deposited, one in the office of the secretary of State, the other in the archives of such city, after being recorded in the office of the recorder of deeds therein. All courts shall take judicial knowledge thereof.

ARTICLE XIII.

Amendment of City Charters.

SECTION 1. Any city charter ratified as aforesaid may be amended by propositions therefor submitted to and passed by the city council of said city, and submitted to the electors thereof at any election held not less than thirty days nor more than sixty days thereafter, and ratified by the vote of a majority of the electors voting thereon at such election, and approved by the general assembly as herein above provided for the approval of city charters.

City charters, how amended.

In submitting any such charter or any amendment thereto, any alternative article may be presented for the choice of the electors, and may be voted for separately without prejudice to any other articles.

ARTICLE XIV.

Division of Towns.

SECTION 1. Any town may be divided into more than one town, or into a city and town, or towns, by causing a board of ten persons who shall have been at least five years electors in said town to be elected by the electors of said town at any election held for that purpose. It shall be the duty of such board to meet, to hold public meetings, to hear the parties interested, and to report a plan to carry out such division to the town council of such town. After publication of such report, as said town council may determine, and after thirty days and within sixty days thereafter, it shall be submitted to the electors of said town at an election held for that purpose. If ratified by a vote of a majority of the electors voting thereon, it shall be submitted to the general assembly for its approval or rejection as a whole, and if approved by the general assembly, it shall become a law.

ARTICLE XV.

Change of Boundaries of Towns and Cities.

Town and city boundaries, how changed.

SECTION 1. The general assembly shall have power to change the boundary lines of towns and cities, provided a majority of the electors living in such territory, as well as of the town or city to which it is to be annexed voting thereon, shall vote therefor, in such manner as the general assembly may determine.

ARTICLE XVI.

Of Town or City Regulations.

Town ordinances.

SECTION 1. Any town or city may make and enforce within its own limits all such ordinances, sanitary, police, and other regulations as are not in conflict with the general laws.

ARTICLE XVII.

On Corporations.

Corporations under control of general assembly.

SECTION 1. The general assembly shall enact, amend, or repeal, as may be necessary from time to time, general laws for the creation, regulation and control of corporations. But no corporation shall be created under any special act.

SEC. 2. Stockholders in corporations created in this State may vote one vote for each share for each person to be elected to office in such corporation, by person or by proxy, or they may cumualte all their votes on one candidate or distribute them among as many candidates as they see fit, as any such corporation may determine. *Voting by stockholders.*

SEC. 3. No corporation shall increase its capital stock, except with the consent of a majority of the stockholders in value at a meeting for such purpose, held after such notice thereof as the general assembly by general law shall determine. *Increase of capital stock.*

SEC. 4. No corporation shall issue preferred stock without the consent of two-thirds of the stockholders in value. *Preferred stock, how issued.*

SEC. 5. The charters of all corporations hereafter created in this State may be altered or repealed by amendment to the constitution of this State or by general law, and no contract shall be created or extended under any charter or act of incorporation or under any amendment of either that shall not be subject to alteration or repeal by the general assembly. *Charters subject to amendment or repeal by general assembly.*

SEC. 6. Whenever hereafter any law shall be passed affecting any corporation existing at the time of the adoption of this constitution, or hereafter created, no such corporation shall be entitled to the benefits thereof, except on condition that such corporation shall thereafter hold its charter subject to the provisions of this constitution; in which case, it shall file an acceptance of such condition with the secretary of State in such manner as the general assembly shall by law determine. *Corporations to file acceptance of provisions of law.*

SEC. 7. No corporation can engage in any business other than that expressly authorized by its charter or the law under which it is formed. *Corporation can transact only the business authorized by its charter.*

SEC. 8. Every corporation organized or doing business in this State, other than religious, educational, or benevolent corporations, and whether domestic corporations or foreign corporations, shall have an office in this State for the transaction of business and an officer or agent therein upon whom service of process may be made, and shall make annual return to the general treasurer of its business in this State. The general assembly shall have power to enforce the provisions of this section by general laws. *Corporations to have an office and agent in this State.*

SEC. 9. No corporation may issue stock or bonds, except for money, labor done, or property at its actual market value, actually received, and after the directors thereof shall have filed their certificate to that effect under oath with the secretary of State.

SEC. 10. Railroads and steamboats are public highways and common carriers, and are therefore subject to reasonable legislative control. The general assembly shall have power to pass laws to correct abuses and prevent unjust discrimination and extortion, and to establish reasonable maximum rates of fare and freight.

SEC. 11. No street railway shall be hereafter constructed in any town or city without the consent in writing of a majority in value of the abutting property owners, nor without the consent of the local town or city council.

SEC. 12. No corporation shall acquire any right in any public highway in any town or city, without the consent of a majority of the electors voting thereon in such town or city, at an election to be held for that purpose, and upon such terms and conditions as may be determined by the council of such town or city granting such privilege. No exclusive privilege shall be granted to any corporation unless confirmed by the vote of a majority of the electors in the town or city in which it is proposed such exclusive privilege shall be granted.

SEC. 13. Stockholders in corporations created in this State shall not be liable for the debts of the corporation, except to the extent of unpaid stock therein owned by them.

SEC. 14. Directors of corporations created in this State shall be jointly and severally liable to creditors and stockholders thereof for all moneys embezzled or misappropriated by the officers or employees thereof during their term of office, and for any false certificate made by them.

SEC. 15. No railroad or other quasi-public corporation shall issue any stock or bonds, except for money, labor, or property actually received and applied to the purposes for which such corporation was created, and all stock, dividends, and other fictitious increase of the capital stock or indebtedness of any such corporation shall be void. The capital stock of such corporations shall not be increased for any

How corporation can issue stock or bonds.

Regulation of transportation corporations.

Consent of abutting owners necessary to construction of street railway.

Consent of electors necessary to corporation.

Acquiring right of way in public highway or exclusive privilege.

Liability of stockholders for debts of corporation.

Liability of directors.

Issue of fictitious capital stock prohibited.

purpose, except after public notice for sixty days, in such manner as may be provided by law.

SEC. 16. No street railway, gas, water, steam heating, telephone, or electric light company, association, or any one carrying on such business within a city or town shall be permitted or authorized to construct its tracks, lay its pipes or mains, or erect its poles, posts, or other apparatus along, over, under, or across the streets, highways, alleys or public grounds of a city or town, without the consent of the city or town council of such city or town being first obtained.

Consent of city or town necessary before rails, &c., can be laid in streets.

SEC. 17. No city or town shall be authorized or permitted to grant any franchise or privilege, or make any contract in reference thereto, for a term exceeding twenty years. Before granting such franchise or privilege for a term of years, such municipality shall first, after due advertisement, receive bids therefor publicly, and award the same to the highest responsible bidder; but it shall have the right to reject any or all bids. This section shall not apply to a trunk railway.

No city or town to grant franchise for more than twenty years, &c.

SEC. 18. No railroad, steamboat, or other common carrier, under heavy penalty to be fixed by the general assembly, shall give a free pass or passes, or shall, at reduced rates not common to the public, sell tickets or transportation to any State, district, city, town, or county officer, or member of the general assembly, or judge; and any State, district, city, town, or county officer, or member of the general assembly, or judge who shall accept or use a free pass or passes, or shall receive or use tickets or transportation at reduced rates not common to the public shall forfeit his office. It shall be the duty of the general assembly to enact laws to enforce the provisions of this section.

Free passes to public officers forbidden.

ARTICLE XVIII.

Of Education.

SECTION 1. It shall be the duty of the general assembly to promote public schools and to adopt all means which it may deem necessary and proper to secure to the people the advantages and opportunities of education.

Duty of general assembly to promote public schools and education.

SEC. 2. The money which now is or which may hereafter be appropriated by law for the establishment of a permanent

Permanent public school fund.

14

fund for the support of public schools shall be securely invested and remain a perpetual fund for that purpose.

Donations for support of public schools. SEC. 3. All donations for the support of public schools or for other purposes of education, which may be received by the general assembly, shall be applied according to the terms prescribed by the donors.

Said fund not to be diverted from said uses. SEC. 4. The general assembly shall not divert said money or fund from the aforesaid uses, nor borrow, appropriate, or use the same, or any part thereof, for any other purpose, under any pretence whatsoever.

Duty of general assembly under this article. SEC. 5. The general assembly shall make all necessary provisions by law for carrying this article into effect.

ARTICLE XIX.

Of Amendments.

Amendments to constitution, how proposed and adopted. SECTION 1. Amendments to this constitution may be proposed in either house of the general assembly, and passed in both houses by a majority of all the members of each house, the ayes and nays being recorded in the journal. Such proposed amendments shall then be submitted to the electors at the next general election, and if approved by a majority of the electors voting thereon shall be declared by the governor to have become a part of this constitution.

ARTICLE XX.

Of Constitutional Conventions.

How the general assembly may call a constitutional convention. SECTION 1. Whenever a majority of the members of both houses vote to call a convention to revise the constitution, the question shall be submitted to the electors at the next general election, and if approved by a majority of the electors voting thereon, the general assembly shall provide for the calling of a convention. Such convention shall consist of delegates equal in number to and elected in the same manner as the members of the general assembly, to be elected at an election to be called for that purpose by the general assembly.

SEC. 2. Whenever   per centum of the people shall petition the general assembly in any one year to call a constitutional convention, the general assembly shall submit to the electors at the next general election the question whether a constitutional convention shall be called, and if a majority of the electors voting thereon shall vote in the affirmative, the general assembly shall forthwith make provision to carry into effect the will of the people thus made manifest, by providing for the election of delegates to such constitutional convention equal in number to, and elected in the same manner as, the members of the general assembly, to be elected at an election to be called for that purpose by the general assembly.

How the people may call a constitutional convention.

SEC. 3. The delegates so elected, under either section one or two hereof, shall meet at the State capitol within four weeks next ensuing after their election, and shall continue in session until their business is completed. No new constitution nor amendment to the constitution shall be submitted for approval to the electors unless by the assent of a majority of all the delegates elected to the convention, the yeas and nays to be entered on their journal. The convention shall determine the rules of its own proceedings, choose its own officers and fix their compensation and the compensation of its own members, and shall be the judge of the election, returns, and qualifications of its own members. In case of any vacancy in its membership, it shall be filled by the town or district by a new election. The new constitution or amendments adopted by such convention shall be submitted to the vote of the electors of the State including those who will become electors thereunder, at the time and in the manner provided by such convention, either as a whole, or section by section or both, as such convention may provide, at an election that shall be held not less than six weeks after the adjournment of the convention. Upon the approval by a majority of the electors voting thereon of such new constitution or amendments, it or they shall go into effect thirty days after said approval, and proclamation thereof shall be made by the governor.

Powers and duties of convention.

ARTICLE XXI.

Of the Adoption of this Constitution.

SECTION 1. The governor, lieutenant-governor, secretary of State, attorney-general, general treasurer, and senators and representatives in the general assembly in office when

General officers and members of assembly at the time of the adoption of

fund for the support … … … shall continue to hold their

vested and remain a p… … … … and subject to the limita-

Donations for support of public schools.

SEC. 3. All donatio… … … officers, until the first

for other purposes of … A. D. … and until their successors

the general assembly, … … … in their number from

terms prescribed by the … … … which is prescribed

Said fund not to be diverted from said uses.

SEC. 4. The general … …

or fund from the aforesa… … … named in the next

use the same, or any p… … … shall be held upon

under any pretence wha… … November, A. D. ,

Duty of general assembly under this article.

SEC. 5. The general … … constitution. The town,

provisions by law for ca… … shall be warned and

… … … … examined, authenticated,

A … … … prescribed by law,

… … their offices from the

Q… … A. D. , until the first

… thereafter until their

Amendments to constitution, how proposed and adopted.

SECTION 1. Amendme… …

posed in either house of … shall provide by law, sub-

both houses by a majorit… …stitution, for the registration

the ayes and nays being … … vote at said first election,

posed amendments shall … the

the next general election … …ple held before said first

the electors voting thereo… , the

to have become a part of … … such as were required

…ting at the time of the

A… … of the supreme court in

Of Constitu… … this constitution shall

… for therein until their

How the general assembly may call a constitutional convention.

SECTION 1. Whenever … … provisions thereof.

houses vote to call a conven… by law at the time

question shall be submitted … continue with their

eral election, and if approv… the new justices

voting thereon, the genera…

calling of a convention. … shall be heard,

delegates equal in number … in the various

ner as the members of the … …ending for the

at an election to be called … … pending.

… all persons

…ever per c… …tion or laws

…nbly in any …

this constitution goes into effect shall continue to hold their offices with the powers and duties, and subject to the limitations, prescribed therein for like officers, until the first Tuesday in January, A. D.   , and until their successors are elected and qualified. Vacancies in their number from any cause shall be filled in the manner which is prescribed by law at the time of their occurrence.

SEC. 2. The first election of officers named in the next preceding section under this constitution shall be held upon the Tuesday after the first Monday in November, A. D.   , by the electors qualified under this constitution. The town, ward, and district meetings therefor shall be warned and conducted, and the result thereof determined, authenticated, and declared in the manner at that time prescribed by law, and the persons then elected shall hold their offices from the said first Tuesday in January, A. D.   , until the first Tuesday in January, A. D.   , and thereafter until their successors are elected and qualified.

SEC. 3. The general assembly shall provide by law, subject to the provisions of this constitution, for the registration necessary to qualify persons to vote at said first election, which registration shall close on the

     . For all elections by the people held before said first Tuesday after the first Monday in   , the qualifications of the electors shall be such as were required by the constitution and laws existing at the time of the adoption of this constitution.

SEC. 4. The three senior justices of the supreme court in office at the time of the adoption of this constitution shall constitute the supreme court provided for therein until their offices are vacated in accordance with the provisions thereof. All courts, as constituted and organized by law at the time of the adoption of this constitution shall continue with their respective jurisdictions and powers until the new justices shall be appointed by the governor.

SEC. 5. All legal proceedings now pending shall be heard, decided, and disposed of as nearly as may be in the various courts constituted hereunder similar to or standing for the courts in which such legal proceedings are now pending.

SEC. 6. Except as herein otherwise provided, all persons who shall hold any office under the constitution or laws

---

Margin notes:

this constitution to hold office until first Tuesday in January, 1900.

First election under this constitution, when to be held.

Registration.

Qualifications of electors.

Supreme court how constituted.

Jurisdiction and powers of courts not to be affected by adoption of this constitution.

Pending litigation not to be affected.

Persons holding certain offices not to

existing at the time of the adoption of this constitution shall continue to hold their offices in the same manner and with the same effect as if it had not been adopted. be affected by the adoption of this constitution.

SEC. 7.   All statutes and resolutions, public and private, not repugnant to this constitution shall continue in force until they expire by their own limitation or are repealed by the general assembly. All charters, contracts, judgments, actions and rights of action shall be as valid as if this constitution had not been made, and all debts contracted and engagements entered into on behalf of the State before this constitution takes effect shall be as valid against the State as if this constitution had not been adopted. Present statutes, etc., to remain in force, until when.
Charters, contracts, judgments, etc., not affected.
Former debts, etc., adopted.

SEC. 8.   All officers who by the provisions of this constitution are continued in office beyond the stated time for which they were elected or appointed shall receive a pro rata compensation for their increased term of service, based upon the compensation provided for in this constitution or by law. Compensation of officers continued in office.

SEC. 9.   This constitution shall take effect upon the proclamation by the governor that it has been duly approved by the people. Constitution to take effect when.

SEC. 10.   No provision of the constitution which has been hereby superseded shall continue in force as a part of the constitutional law of the State except so far as it is re-affirmed in this constitution. Provisions of old constitution to continue in force, to what extent.

SEC. 11.   For the purpose of submission to the electors, said proposition shall be designated "THE NEW CONSTITUTION OF THE STATE OF RHODE ISLAND AND PROVIDENCE PLANTATIONS." Proposition, how designated.

SEC. 12.   The said new constitution and any future amendments or new constitution shall be submitted to the electors who will become the electors thereunder for their approval or rejection, at meetings of the electors to be held on the   , in the words following, to wit :—"Shall 'The new constitution (or amendments to the constitution, as the case may be) of the State of Rhode Island and Providence Plantations' be adopted?"   The voting places in the several cities and towns shall be kept open during the hours required by law for voting therein for general officers of the State. Proposed new constitution to be voted on.

SEC. 13.   The secretary of State shall cause this new constitution to be published in the manner provided by law for publishing the public laws of the State, prior to the day of the said meetings of the said electors; and the said proposition Publication of proposition.

shall be inserted by the town and city clerks in the warrants or notices by them to be issued previous to said meetings of the electors for the purpose of warning the town, ward, or district meetings; and said proposition shall be read by the town, ward, and district clerks to the electors in the town, ward, and district meetings to be held as aforesaid.

Town, ward, and district meetings, how warned. SEC. 14. The town, ward, and district meetings to be held as aforesaid shall be warned, and the list of voters shall be canvassed and made up, and the said town, ward, and district meetings shall be conducted in the same manner as now provided by law for the town, ward, and district meetings for the election of general officers of the State.

Counting and certifying of ballots cast. SEC. 15. At the close of the polls on said day of said meetings of the electors, the moderator and town clerk, or the warden and ward clerk, or the moderator and district clerk shall, in open town, ward, or district meeting, count said ballots and seal up the same, and shall certify that the ballots by them sealed up are the ballots given in at said meetings of the electors, the number of such ballots, and that the number of ballots on said proposition does not exceed the number of electors voting at said meetings, what number of persons voted and how many ballots there are, and shall deliver or send such ballots, so sealed up and certified, to the secretary of State within five days after said   day of   , A. D. 18 .

Official count and proclamation of result. SEC. 16. The governor, secretary of State, and attorney-general shall count said ballots on or before the   day of   , A. D. 18 . And the governor shall announce the result by proclamation, on or before the   day of   , A. D. 18 , and if said new constitution shall have been approved by a majority of the electors of the State present and voting thereon in said town, ward, and district meetings, the same shall be declared to be "THE CONSTITUTION OF THE STATE OF RHODE ISLAND AND PROVIDENCE PLANTATIONS."

ANALYTICAL INDEX.

114

CPSIA information can be obtained
at www.ICGtesting.com
Printed in the USA
BVHW040911211218
536170BV00015B/339/P